NO REGRETS

Ben and Mecca *(Dorothy Reitman)*

NO REGRETS

Dr. Ben Reitman and
the Women Who Loved Him

A Biographical Memoir

Mecca Reitman Carpenter

SouthSide Press
LEXINGTON

Cover and interior design: Abacus Graphics, Oceanside, CA
Printed in the United States of America on acid-free paper

Published by SouthSide Press
94 Pleasant Street
Lexington, MA 02421
(800) 378-8711

Publisher's Cataloging-in-Publication
(*Provided by Quality Books, Inc.*)

Carpenter, Mecca Reitman
      No regrets : Dr. Ben Reitman and the women who loved him/
Mecca Reitman Carpenter.
      p. cm.
      Includes bibliographical references.
      Preassigned LCCN: 97-91152

      1. Reitman, Ben L. (Ben Lewis), 1879-1942. 2. Goldman,
Emma, 1869-1940--Relations with men. 3. Social reformers--
Chicago--Biography. 4. Reitman, Ben L. (Ben Lewis), 1879-1942
--Relations with women.   I. Title.

HN80.C5C37 1999   303.4'84'092
                            QBI95-20811

ISBN 0-9650584-0-9
First Edition

*A selection from THE PROPHET by Kahil Gibran, copyright 1923 by Kahil
Gibran and renewed 1951 by Administrators C T A of Kahil Gibran Estate and
Mary G. Gibran, is reprinted by permission of Alfred A. Knopf Inc.*

To my sisters
Medina, Victoria and Olive

When love beckons to you, follow him
Though his ways are hard and steep.
And when his wings enfold you yield to him,
Though the sword hidden among his pinions may wound
  you.
And when he speaks to you believe in him,
Though his voice may shatter your dreams as the north
  wind lays waste the garden.
For even as love crowns you so shall he crucify you.
Even as he is for your growth so is he for your pruning.
Even as he ascends to your height and caresses your
  tenderest branches that quiver in the sun,
So shall he descend to your roots and shake them in their
  clinging to the earth. . . .
All these things shall love do unto you that you may know
  the secrets of your heart, and in that knowledge become
  a fragment of Life's heart.
But if in your fear you would seek only love's peace and
  love's pleasure,
Then it is better for you that you cover your nakedness
  and pass out of love's threshing floor.

  —From The Prophet *by Kahlil Gibran*

There is only one positive proof I have that God loves me
and there's really something to me, and it's the fact that so
many worthwhile women have loved me and been kind to
me, and have given me their best and their all.

  —Ben Reitman to Leonard Abbott, 1940

Dr. Ben Reitman and
the Women Who Loved Him

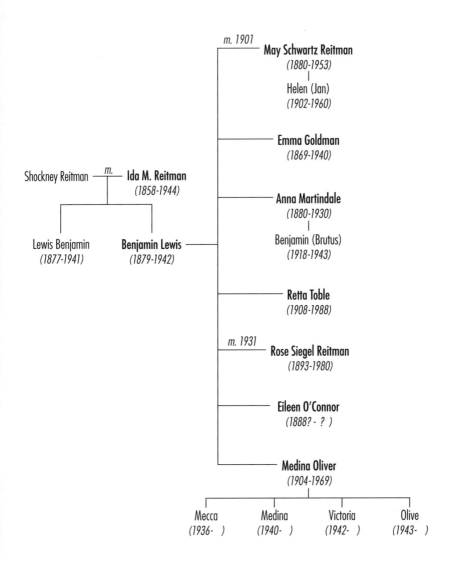

m. 1901

May Schwartz Reitman
(1880-1953)

Helen (Jan)
(1902-1960)

Emma Goldman
(1869-1940)

Shockney Reitman — *m.* — **Ida M. Reitman**
(1858-1944)

Anna Martindale
(1880-1930)

Benjamin (Brutus)
(1918-1943)

Lewis Benjamin
(1877-1941)

Benjamin Lewis
(1879-1942)

Retta Toble
(1908-1988)

m. 1931

Rose Siegel Reitman
(1893-1980)

Eileen O'Connor
(1888? - ?)

Medina Oliver
(1904-1969)

Mecca
(1936-)

Medina
(1940-)

Victoria
(1942-)

Olive
(1943-)

Contents

Acknowledgments

Writing this book would not have been possible without my family. In addition to the thanks I owe my mother and father for saving their papers, I am also indebted to living relatives. Dorothy Reitman, my sister-in-law, deserves major credit for preserving my father's papers and for her generosity in sharing her private collection of letters with me. My sister, Medina Gross, started me moving through time and feeling with the boxes of family letters she had saved (and I had been willing to throw out) after our mother's death. Medina's help continued for the entire project. My sisters, Olive Poliks and Victoria Kapp, were also generous with their papers and thoughts. Herb Gross, Ed Kapp and Jerry Poliks were encouraging. Rhoda Reitman Kuster and Ruth Reitman Highberg shared their photographs and stories of "Uncle Ben." Eugene and Peggy Oliver provided materials and answered questions about their side of my family. Charles Gay, a relative of my half-sister, Jan Gay, gave new life to my research when it languished.

The help and intellectual stimulation of the Reitman and Goldman scholars, Suzanne Poirier, Roger Bruns, Candace Falk, Alice Wexler, Alix Kates Shulman and Elmer Gertz, are most gratefully acknowledged. Suzanne Poirier has been a friend and Chicago connection. Elmer Gertz gave me permission to use his unpublished biography of Ben. Lila Weinberg and Mamie Gertz told me their stories. Discussions with Hildegarde Duane, Sister Helen Szekely and Donald Schwartz were insightful. Ruth Surgal provided Reitman letters and photographs and she and Peter Leibundguth channeled material to the University of Illinois at Chicago.

A number of library archives held invaluable resources. My appreciation to the staff of Special Collections, The University Library, University of Illinois at Chicago cannot be overstated. In working my way through the voluminous Ben L. Reitman Papers, Mary Ann Bamberger, Assistant Special Collections Librarian, and her staff, including Zita Stukas and Terry Moon, were helpful repeatedly. My father's legacy could not have better guardian angels.

Other sources were the Emma Goldman Collection, Special Collections, Boston University; the Emma Goldman Collection, International Institute for Social History, Amsterdam; the Theodore Schroeder Papers, Special Collections/Morris Library, Southern Illinois University, Carbondale; the Emma Goldman Papers Project, University of California, Berkeley; and Special Collections, University of Chicago Library.

I am deeply indebted to a number of people who generously gave me their time and expertise in editing my manuscript in different stages. The mistakes remain my own. Thank you to Barbara Keller, Rudena Mallory, Peter Bochner, Arthur Levin, Frank O'Toole, Sandra Ortiz, Lori Brandt, Ken Swezey, Cindy Victor, Roger Bruns, Suzanne Poirier, Connie Bullock, CarolAnn Moore, Kristi Dalven, Harley Freeman, Pat Ford, Laurel Carpenter, Holly Carpenter, Carol Elliott, Lynn Coppel, Sunni Boyd, Marsha Edwards, Denny Price, Patti-Jean Samson and Carol Amato.

Special thanks also to Barbara Kozick, my secretary and friend, whose skill and patience took me through many versions of the manuscript. Lucy Parker designed the first draft of the cover and gave me confidence I would have a book. Suzanne Eiler, Barbara Keller, Ani Markarian, Aida Morad, Marilyn Oropeza, Georgia Thornton, Judy Sterling and Angela Barker also contributed ideas. Linda Christensen verified dates. Richard Wentworth provided editorial advice and was generous in other ways. Claudia Suzanne was a mentor and guide as well as my editor.

Finally, the multifaceted support of my husband, Alden, over many years, allowed me to follow in some of my father's footsteps.

Author's Note

I have taken the liberty of correcting my father's spelling and punctuation and, to a lesser extent, that of his correspondents. Part of the charm is lost, but it does make their letters easier to read.

Prologue

In the spring of 1913, the fiery revolutionary Emma Goldman and my father, her comrade lover, took the train to San Diego as part of Emma's national speaking tour. Warned by local radicals not to come, they expected to confront the "law and order" vigilantes who had tortured and "tarred and sage-brushed" my father the previous year when they were there on a similar mission.

Emma and my father were arrested as soon as they stepped off the train. From their jail cells they could hear the shouts of the vigilantes in the street—"Reitman! We want Reitman!"—followed by the honking of automobile horns and the shriek of police sirens. "They could not forgive him for returning. They wanted his life!" Emma later remembered.

This time Emma wanted to stay and face the crowd, but my father refused. To Emma, his decision was the ultimate act of cowardice. "The pale horror staring at me out of Ben's eyes made me realize the meaning of fear as I had never seen it before," she later recalled.

When they left the jail for the train station, their police escorts stood on the running boards of the car with their rifles pointed out into the crowd. "Our appearance was greeted with savage howls. There was a swaying jostling human pack . . . drunk with the lust of blood," Emma remembered. She and Ben boarded the train, but before it pulled out, the man who had led the attack on my father the previous year broke through the barricade of policemen, rushed forward, and spat in my father's face.

Emma never forgave my father, and her letters often reminded him that he was a coward. Even that was not enough. "I grieved to realize that Ben was not of heroic stuff," she wrote in her autobiography almost twenty years later. "He was not the texture of Sasha [her life-long comrade, Alexander Berkman], who had courage enough for a dozen men and extraordinary coolness and presence of mind in moments of danger."

Just reading Emma's description of the San Diego riot frightens me. My father was right in choosing life. Emma's brave comrade Sasha had tried to murder a man for a political cause. For all my father's talk on soapboxes about bombs and the Revolution, he loved life, not only his own, but that of others. Professionally and philosophically, he was committed to healing and living.

I Have Never Denied
Any of the Charges

I have been called in private, on the platform, in articles and in books, a liar, a thief, a cheat, a pimp, an adulterer, a robber of innocent women, a drunkard, a dope fiend, a pervert, a hypocrite, a four flusher, a bastard, a cheap organism, a socialist, an anarchist, a communist, a stool pigeon, an agent provocateur, an army deserter, a jailbird, and an ex-convict, a gangster, a bootlegger, an underworld type. A friend and pal of murderers, thieves and crooks also. I have been called a renegade Christian, a disloyal revolutionist, a cowardly radical and almost every name that one can label or discredit a man.

I HAVE NEVER DENIED any of the charges.

—*Ben Reitman to his wife Rose, 1934*

M y father, Benjamin Lewis Reitman, M.D., died in 1942 at sixty-three, worn out from a life of compassionate service, frustrated idealism, and frank disregard for his own health. Whether the sins he described in his letter to Rose contributed to his early demise or added to his longevity is a matter of interpretation. Blended into the mix was his immense joy in the adventure of being alive and his splendid ability to convey this joy in life and in his letters.

Emma Goldman's version of her relationship with my father is the most exciting, the most passionate, the most widely known, and, by far, the most damning to his character, of any of my father's love stories. Fortunately for me, there were other women who told different versions of him in their love stories. In addition to the passionate crusader Emma, there was the quiet idealist Anna; the furious Rose, who fought to reform him; the shy spinster Eileen; my rebellious mother Medina; and other women who left a shorter written record, or no record at all. My father's relationships with all these women, and with his jealous mother, Ida—along with most of his life's work—remained a well-kept family secret while I was growing up.

The only love story I knew as a child was my mother's: how she and my father met on West Madison Street in Chicago and fell in love, their long "courtship," their sweet "marriage" vows, and their short but happy life together that produced their finest life's dream—my sisters and me. This love story also bore the strong but unspoken message that I shouldn't try to know more.

It was not until after my mother's death in 1969 that I had an inkling this favorite story from my childhood was not what it seemed. Looking back now, I see many clues, but a week after my mother's funeral, I encountered the first evidence I was unable to ignore.

One of my sisters called from Chicago to tell me that the will was being probated in the judge's private chambers. It had been arranged, she said, by Art Main, our lawyer and cousin, because "Momma and Poppa weren't married."

Although I would later be amused by my illegitimacy and feel special, my first response was shock. I was thirty-three. My father had been dead since I was six. My mother had always told us what a wonderful man he was.

"Why didn't anyone say anything?" I asked my sister. "If Art knew, all the Reitmans must have known. Did Grandma know? Did all our relatives in Texas know?" These questions were too late for my grandmother, semiconscious in a nursing home in Houston.

"I don't know," was all my sister answered. Silence followed. The idea seemed incredible to both of us, but possible.

Given this startling news, I took the action I had been trained for from childhood: I did nothing. I didn't want to know more. My life seemed full. Why look back? It would take almost twenty years before I was finally ready to reject my mother's intense desire for secrecy and accept both the pain and the rewards of separating Ben Reitman, the man, from my father, the family legend.

Fortunately, as I approached fifty, newly published material, first about Emma Goldman and then about Ben, aroused my dormant interest in my father. This, in turn, drew me with excitement to dust-covered boxes of family letters my sisters had stored. Reading these books and letters in mid-life—and a strong sense of unfinished business—gave me the energy to tackle the immense volumes of my father's papers in the library archives at the University of Illinois at Chicago. As my information began to accumulate, even more boxes of letters surfaced. Previously ignored clues from my early life also began to reveal further secrets about my father.

Few daughters have the chance to read their father's seduction of their mother's rival by mail fifty years after the fact. Fewer still would want it! But when the opportunity came in a long-packed-away box of family letters, I took it with deep appreciation. Eventually I grew to love the rival, Eileen.

But the more I came to know my father and the women in his life, the more I saw common elements in the women's love stories: much was omitted; some things were falsified (consciously or unconsciously); and the heroine of each story saw herself at center stage, regardless of who else might be waiting in the wings. My father's written commentary both about his own life and about these women adds a fascinating counterpoint.

In one of the letters, I found a message from my father to me, a scrap of paper placed in a bottle and thrown into the ocean of time. Shortly before I was born, my father wrote to my then eighteen-year-old half-brother Brutus about his hopes for me:

> And I'm hoping that Mecca, when she arrives, will want to know me.
> Yes, when the smoke has cleared away, when the toxins have been neutralized,
> I am so happy, so glad to be alive, so proud of my Children, Mother, Medina
> And myself. Yes I have loved "it all." No regrets, no mistakes, no accidents.

Long after I had started my research about my father, a woman asked me how I could love such a terrible man. Many women who preceded me had been asked exactly the same question. This book is my answer.

TWO

I Will Be Remembered
By My Carbons

My time on earth is limited. What will become of my little babies and what will become of Mother? I place no burdens on you, my son. I believe in Medina, that if she lives she will be able to take care of her babies. And if she dies . . . Then what? We shall see. That is one reason I am so anxious to keep up my insurance.

—*Ben Reitman to his son, Brutus, 1941*

Knowing those difficult years both before and after my father's death makes it easy to understand my mother now. The painful parts of loving Ben were largely winnowed out. Instead, she kept what she needed to sustain herself through the hardship of holding her family together.

"There was a struggle before the children; life has been a struggle since the children; even more problems have come since my husband's death which I feel less capable of solving than before," my mother wrote four years after my father died. "As long as there is life there is change—the struggle is to enjoy."

The problems my mother alluded to began immediately after Ben's death in November 1942. My father had willed the house, his literary works, and all his effects to his son Brutus, but he left one legacy to my mother: a last pregnancy. Twenty years later, she recalled to my youngest sister, Olive, that she cried all during that pregnancy. "It seemed as though all of life's sadness came at once and if I hadn't had you, the period would have been much worse and sadder," she wrote. Barely six, I could have offered little comfort or even help in caring for my sisters, Medina and Victoria, then two and one.

At the time of my father's death, Brutus, then an Army Air Corps lieutenant, was living with his young wife, Dorothy, in Detroit. After the funeral in Chicago, Brutus and Dorothy hurriedly packed up and stored the contents of my father's office, including voluminous files containing manuscripts, reports, newspaper clippings, and correspondence.

Brutus returned to active duty but, a month later, became so ill with the measles that he was hospitalized over Christmas. He returned to flight duty before full recovery. Unrecognized by his physicians was another medical complication: the precursor to spinal meningitis. While transporting a plane alone from Detroit to a Southern base, he was forced by ill health to make an emergency landing in a farm field. The loyal son whom my father thought would practice medicine and assume his family responsibilities, the loving older brother for her children that my mother would remember so affectionately, the passionate and adored young husband whom Dorothy thought would always take care of her, could not fulfill his promises. Twenty-five-year-old Brutus died a week later in early 1943. He and Dorothy were expecting their first child.

Dorothy was now my father's legal heir. Given a new baby on the way and her own family's limited resources, Dorothy was encouraged by her mother to move quickly to claim the rest of my father's estate. The story of my mother hiding a few of my father's books and papers at a neighbor's house the night before Dorothy and her mother came to take away his things became one of our family's most vivid and often-told tales.

Of course, we had no way of knowing that this source of

my mother's distress would be the bridge to history for my father. Devoted to Brutus and in awe of her father-in-law, Dorothy stored the bulk of my father's papers, largely intact, for almost thirty years. "I will be remembered by my carbons," my father prophetically wrote a friend. Dorothy made my father's vision possible.

Some of my father's papers remained scattered among our possessions. Our crayon scribbles on the backs of letters suggest why there might be many missing.

By the time my father's will was probated, our modest house remained the only thing of value. True to form, Ben had borrowed to the limits of his creditors. After his death, they took what could be liquidated. "He hadn't paid the rent on his office for years," was Dorothy's understatement.

But my father's efforts to keep up his insurance policies were his investment in our future. My mother obtained a court order allowing her to use the insurance money my sisters and I inherited to purchase the house from Dorothy. Staying in the house my mother and father had shared gave stability to our lives during this difficult period.

For many months, my mother was unable to face her own mother with the news of her pregnancy and Ben's death. For a while she held two jobs until the canning factory where she worked evenings as a nurse fired her for sleeping on the job. Finally, out of total desperation, she wrote for help.

What was in the letter to her mother I do not know, but very likely it contained what my grandmother Inez Oliver called my mother's "marriage certificate." My grandmother kept the paper in her safety deposit box until the end of her life. My uncle Gene Oliver gave it to me when I was starting my research. When I unfolded it, I saw it was my father's death certificate which listed Medina Oliver Reitman as his wife.

I'm sure my grandmother wanted to believe my mother and father were married, particularly once he was dead.

Perhaps that tenuous evidence was sufficient. My mother's name and our names were now Reitman for her. In the thirty years I knew her afterwards, she never once suggested otherwise. Despite my mother's full-time work as a nurse for the rest of her life, it was my grandmother Oliver's financial and moral support that made it possible for my mother to hold our family together.

My Reitman grandmother, Ida, who had been living with my father and mother, went to stay with Dorothy after Brutus' death, moving on to a nursing home for her final year of life. She was buried in what is still an unmarked grave in Chicago. After her two sons and grandson were gone, there was no woman in her life who cared enough to buy a headstone for her.

THREE

Ida's Son

My obsession with my mother has continued; although
she is seventy and I am more than fifty, there is a bond
between us that is more than mother and son. Make your
own deductions. Every man ought to be faithful to at
least one woman—I have chosen my mother.
                    —Ben Reitman to Emma Goldman, 1929

Of all the significant women in my father's life, my grandmother Ida Reitman is one of the few who did not leave a
written record of her love story: she could neither read nor
write. My knowledge of her relationship with my father and
of my father's early days comes from his letters and autobiography and from comments about her by rivals and relatives.
All these sources portray a woman the polar opposite of my
educated, fiercely independent, and rigidly moral Grandmother Oliver. Grandma Reitman depended totally on Ben
and his older brother Lew for support. Moreover, she had
expected them to help support her from the time they were
small boys.

Cousins tell me Ida loved to cook and was a quiet
hostess—at least on formal occasions. In exchange, she jealously guarded her position as queen of Ben's home and
kitchen. A defeated rival, Emma Goldman, wrote bitterly of
her experience with Ida in as early as 1913:

In Chicago she had lived among her pots and kettles,
untouched by the stream outside. She loved her son and she

was always most patient with his moods, no matter how irrational they were. He was her idol who could do no wrong. As to his numerous affairs with women, she was sure it was they who had led her child astray. . . . Ben's mother was always respectful when she met me but I could sense her keen dislike.

Ida was far less polite to Emma's successors. When Brutus visited an old friend of Ben's in Europe in the early 1930s, he wrote his father that his hostess "still remembers the time Gran threw her out of the house." The only kind thing my mother ever said about Ida was that she made good matzo ball soup.

A son's "obsession" with his mother is a classic story and from the beginning Ben and Ida had a strong affinity. Later, Ben greatly admired Ida for her resourcefulness in holding the family together when she was a poor young immigrant divorcee in the early 1880s. In turn, she had an enduring belief that nothing Ben did was wrong.

Ben wrote sporadically of his early life in his letters, but his fullest description is in his unpublished autobiography, "Following the Monkey" written around 1925. He chose the title from his first boyhood adventure following an organ-grinder's monkey.

Ben cautions the reader about the work's reliability: "A man who began life as I did, surrounded by poverty, ignorance, brutality, and a code of expediency could not expect to be very accurate in his reminiscences." But even if he embellishes his mother's character, the major events are correct. My father's biographer, Roger Bruns, told me he was able to verify many events in Ben's autobiography that other men might be tempted to omit.

Looking back, Ben saw his unconventional early life as an asset. He wrote to a friend, "I was lucky. Came from a broken home." His father, mother, and maternal grandparents were

Eastern European Jews who arrived in this country with the waves of other immigrants in the 1870s. When the family arrived in St. Paul, Minnesota, his father, Shockney Reitman, and his Grandfather Levinson were in business together as tramp peddlers, selling dry goods and notions to isolated farm families. Lewis Benjamin, known in the family as Lew, was born in 1877. Benjamin Lewis was born on January 1, 1879. The spelling was later changed to Louis.

Ida was protective of Ben from early childhood; she told him later he was a sickly child who required special care. When Ben was one and his brother three, Shockney abandoned the marginal business and his family to make a new life for himself in New York. Shockney provided no further support to the family, and he and Ida were later divorced. Ben often referred to his father's attitude toward family responsibility as a precedent for his own.

Ida's mother died soon after Shockney's desertion, leaving Ida and her two boys to travel with her father and brother, who were peddling goods across the South. When her father moved to New York and remarried, Ida and her sons left for Cleveland, very likely with her father's encouragement. In his autobiography Ben suggested that his grandfather's behavior towards his mother was also a model for him.

At first, the responsibility seemed overwhelming to the young woman; Ida applied to have her three- and five-year-old sons admitted to a Jewish orphanage. But when another charitable organization offered her a ticket to Chicago before the boys could be admitted, she decided to take it.

On their arrival in Chicago, Ida took a cheap room in the red-light district. Through odd jobs, sporadic donations from her father and brother, money from boarders (possibly also the "occasional husbands" my father referred to once in a letter), and frequent moves to escape bill collectors, the family scraped by. As a child, Ben earned pennies fetching beer for neighborhood criminals and laborers. But he was far more impressed with the generous and lighthearted neighborhood prostitutes, who paid him nickels or quarters to run their errands. His warm relationship with this group of women would continue throughout his professional life.

Young Ben and the other poor children in the neighborhood also hunted for coal along the railroad tracks, and picked up bottles in the alleys that could be resold for cash. One winter day when the supply of coal along the tracks was not enough to fill his homemade wagon, eleven-year-old Ben and some other boys climbed on the railroad cars and threw off some coal. A railroad official soon put a stop to this activity.

Ben remembered with pride that this was the first of his many arrests by the railroad police. He was taken to jail and placed in a cell (with several other small children) until his mother came to get him. He recalled that on the walk home from jail, his mother spoke to him kindly, but warned him not to steal coal or anything else. "Better that we freeze than my little son go to jail for stealing coal." If Ida truly made that statement, I'm sure it was a mixed message to her son. The family needed a continuous supply of coal, and Ben or Lew had to get it—somehow.

Ben's early playground was the railroad tracks. He started to ride boxcars when he was still so small he had to be boosted aboard by the older boys. His rides increasingly took him farther from home. But his talent at begging—"Please lady, I'm lost and hungry. I live at 16th Street. Will you give me a glass of water?"—was rewarded with food and carfare so often that it gave him confidence to continue.

Although Ida remarried, Ben mentioned his stepfather only once in his autobiography. Even with a man in the house, there were still no rules or restrictions at home. Ben continued to play hooky from school and ride the railroad cars, and Ida was always willing to come to school to explain his truancies.

Like his older brother, Ben left school permanently at age ten and took a series of odd jobs. Unlike Lew, however, Ben was not ready for responsibility. By age twelve, he made his first major trip as a hobo, riding the rails from Chicago to as far away as Cleveland. When the runaway returned home a few days later, Ben recalled that his mother welcomed him back and gave him a delicious dinner without a scolding. This pattern of unconditional love and "good Jewish cooking" from Ida would persist throughout his life. He wrote of his first adventure, "The homecoming was joyous, but it was short. The spirit of the road was in my blood. I was now an experienced traveler."

Along with many other men and boys at the end of the century, Ben embraced hobo life, despite unsympathetic railroad police, the brutality of the hobo jungle, the uncertainty of food and shelter, and the ever-present danger of injury or death from moving railroad cars. He traveled by rail back and forth across the United States, returning periodically to Chicago to see his mother and to work at odd jobs, including one as an office boy for the Cook Remedy Company, which sold a treatment for syphilis.

On one trip to Florida, Ben impulsively took a job as a fireman on board the tramp steamer *Tresco*. He intended to visit seaports around the world, but after his second watch in the stokehole, he went to the first engineer and said he was quitting. A few kicks and a drenching with a hose, to the cheers of the crew, sent Ben back to his job. He commented later, "I made a speedy recovery, physically and mentally, and as I have done all my life, set about to enjoy life, and make the best out of my unpleasant situation."

He adapted so well that after the *Tresco* reached Europe, he signed on again for a voyage that took him to ports in Africa and Asia before returning to Marseilles. However, his experience in France reinforced the advantages of begging over working. He was so talented at panhandling American tourists in Paris that he was able to make enough in one week to pay his passage to New York.

Ben was fascinated by his fellow hoboes, and years later described them in his poetry and other writings. He admired their need for freedom and their willingness to teach a younger man about life. He was also nonjudgmental about their cruelty. Robbing the defenseless and wounding or killing each other in drunken brawls were just part of the outcast's way of life. Ben strongly believed that through divine intervention, he had been saved from the fate of the outcast's life for a greater purpose.

My father's unpublished autobiography provides insight into the development of his attitudes about sex and religion. For a man whose prolific correspondence is so open about his sexual activities, "Following the Monkey" is curiously limited. This omission may have been Ben's choice, or may have been due to the prospective publisher's fear of anti-obscenity laws.

On Ben's first visit to a hobo jungle, he recalled that the men spoke bitterly about women—characteristic, he wrote, "of all men who have been brutal, unfair and unkind to women." These men would serve as early role models. His early contact with women appears limited to the "motherly" bar girls who were willing to talk to him about their trade, and to the prostitutes in Europe, Africa, and Asia who were patronized by the crew of the *Tresco*.

Although Ben was ambivalent on the subject of homosexuality in most of his writing, he was frank in a largely autobiographical manuscript, "Living with Social Outcasts," written in 1933. He recounted his own homosexual experiences as a twelve-year-old hobo with a sailor in New York, and a more traumatic attempted gang rape in a Virginia barn by "a mob of crooks who were working the State Fair." The men threw him out of the hayloft when he objected. Ben accepted the brutal side of sexuality—along with its joyful side—as a normal part of life. His only comment: "I was a wiser if not a better boy for the experience."

In contrast to his sexuality, Ben covers his religious development in great detail in his autobiography, possibly because "no other part of my philosophy or mental makeup has been questioned or criticized more than my religion." A Jew raised in a nonpracticing family, Ben began attending Protestant Sunday School after he heard the local church was giving away free candy at Christmas. He believed in the power of prayer at an early age, using it whenever he needed anything, including an empty boxcar to sleep in. He carried a Bible with him on his hobo trips and read from it daily most of his life. In addition to whatever spiritual comfort it offered him, it had another benefit: it made railroad officials more friendly.

Following an emotional religious conversion in a New York Bowery mission at age seventeen, my father strongly believed that God had chosen him to help others and to teach them the way to a better world. Later in life, he would be called blasphemous on many occasions by more orthodox Christians, and even I find his use of religious expressions in seduction particularly devious and hypocritical. Nevertheless, my father considered himself a religious person. "My religious life may be a mystery to others but to me it is perfectly clear. They are mystified because to them religion is piety, morality and inhibition. To me religion is love and service."

FOUR

From Medical School to the Hobo College

I had a very difficult time the first year. I not only had to learn anatomy, physiology, and chemistry, but I had to learn reading, writing, and spelling. I got by somehow and passed all my examinations.

—*From "Following the Monkey," 1925*

In 1899 Ben returned home from his travels. Now twenty, he took a position, first as a janitor and then as a laboratory assistant, in the Chicago Polyclinic, working for Dr. Maximilian Herzog. Ben learned the more complicated tasks quickly and, typical of his entire life, made both friends and enemies among the doctors at the clinic. Dr. Herzog thought him so promising he encouraged him to study medicine. Ben also made a lifelong friend of Dr. William Evans, an instructor at the Polyclinic who would later become commissioner of Chicago's Board of Health. Evans would be Ben's benefactor throughout his professional career.

One of the physicians wrote the following letter of recommendation for Ben's admission to medical school: "Ben Reitman . . . has done very fine work, and gives great promise as an original investigator and physician. I am sure that anything he lacks in elemental education, he will make up in zeal and native ability. I urge you to accept him as a medical student." Another doctor wrote grudgingly, "This is to certify that Ben Reitman has been a janitor at the Polyclinic."

My father entered medical school at the College of Physicians and Surgeons (now the University of Illinois College of Medicine) in the fall of 1900 after one of the physicians at the Polyclinic volunteered to pay his tuition. Lew (and possibly Ben's stepfather) supported the family, but Ben earned what he could selling study aids to his fellow medical students. His wares included dogs he picked up on the street—both pets and strays—and skeletons he made by boiling cadavers discarded after dissection. He continued working part-time in the laboratory and, as an upper-classman, taught medical and dental classes.

Ben had his first narrow escape from marriage during his freshman year in medical school. When he was twenty-one, he proposed to a young woman he met in Sunday School (always one of his most productive hunting grounds). But when, just prior to the ceremony, he became instantly infatuated with the minister's sister, he changed his mind. He stopped the service by pretending a fit, making a leap at the minister, and biting him on the neck.

Unfortunately for his bride, my father did not escape so easily the next time. In the summer of 1901, he married May Schwartz, a young musician. Later he wrote that he had never loved May or wanted to get married, but after "a short moony spoony romance," May was "apprehensive and insistent." May's mother was also anxious that they marry and gave the bride $500 for a honeymoon trip to Europe. Ben and May toured Europe for several weeks—then he left her in Prague with less than $200, not knowing she had become pregnant. After a hobo tour of the Continent, he sailed directly for home at the end of the summer. May remained in Prague, expecting him to return.

May traveled from Prague to Germany to continue her musical studies. When their daughter Helen was born, May became so distraught that she was admitted to a German mental sanitarium through the assistance of the local American consulate. May Reitman probably had a history of mental illness prior to her marriage, but her predicament would have shaken almost any woman and could easily have triggered a relapse.

My father claimed he did not know about his new daughter until he went to see May in the sanitarium the following summer, but the news left him totally indifferent. He put his wife and baby daughter on a boat for America and continued hoboing around Great Britain. He returned to America as a stowaway in time for the 1902 fall term at medical school. May and the baby returned to live with her family, and Ben provided no further support for them. Despite May's attempts at reconciliation, she and Ben were divorced in 1905. He had almost no contact with Helen until, as a twenty-year-old college student, she hitchhiked to Chicago in 1922 to meet him and attend one of his lectures.

Although my father's life was characterized, he said, by no regrets, his early abandonment of his daughter was one of the very few exceptions. After he and Helen came to know each other later, he wanted her to love him. They stayed in contact for the rest of his life, even though she often felt bitter towards him. Even during their best periods, there was never the closeness he felt with his son Brutus. He wrote Helen after I was born:

> Mecca is a genuine pure joy to me. Everything I denied you
>   I give her so freely.
> I have often wondered about that. Your mother never
>   harmed me. There never were
> Quarrels or misunderstandings. The desertion was as
> Brutal as it was spontaneous.
> Now after nearly 40 years I cannot understand it.
> I can understand your attitude towards me and justify
>   anything you do.

Of all the women's stories in my father's life, the one of May and her baby has always struck me as the saddest. Most of the women were more than able to take care of themselves. These two were the most defenseless.

May Reitman played only a minor role in Ben's life after their divorce. Once Helen was on her own, May moved to Chicago where she spent many of her remaining years in mental institutions. During the Depression years, when she was not institutionalized, she often came to Ben's office to ask for a few dollars. Her letters to Ben were always deferential and friendly and occasionally enclosed their daughter's correspondence. My mother's only story to me about May was that she would call our house and ask for Ben, identifying herself as *the* Mrs. Reitman.

In 1903, at the end of Ben's junior year, he was expelled from medical school after he was caught arranging for one of his classmates to take a surgery examination for him (a common practice in the early days of American medical training, but hardly excusable). With my father's uncanny knack for making the best of a bad situation, he appealed to Dr. John Dill Robertson, then president of the nearby American College of Medicine and Surgery (later the Loyola School of Medicine), for admission to his school. Robertson, who later succeeded William Evans as commissioner of the Chicago Board of Health, would also be Ben's benefactor many times during his medical career. Admitted to the new school, Ben later wrote, "I had a very happy year at school, worked hard, lived from hand to mouth, taught a little, shot craps, and went out bumming with the boys, passed all my examinations in a credible way, and graduated."

After completing medical school in 1904, the new Dr. Reitman opened a small office at 39th and Cottage Grove. His first patients were from the segment of society he would always feel closest to: the nearby prostitutes, hoboes, criminals and other "outcasts." However, Ben soon found medical practice confining. He would periodically close his practice and leave for hobo trips across the United States, Europe, or Mexico.

It was during his travels after medical school that my father discovered he had an insatiable hunger for publicity and that newspaper reporters considered him good copy. This mutual attraction lasted the rest of his life. Ben began carrying his growing scrapbook of newspaper clippings with him whenever he traveled. When he arrived in a strange town, he would look up a local newspaper editor and say, "I'm Ben Reitman. I'm good for a story. Here, look over my scrapbook."

Over the years, his standard statement to the press became, "I am an American by birth, a Jew by parentage, a Baptist by adoption, single by good fortune, a physician and teacher by profession, cosmopolitan by choice, a socialist by inclination, a rascal by nature, a celebrity by accident, a tramp by twenty years' experience and a tramp reformer." They would print it over and over again.

My father's lifelong interest in hobo welfare and social reform began in 1907. While he was riding the rails through St. Louis, he met the founder of the International Brotherhood Welfare Association, the "millionaire hobo," James Eads How. How had started an early form of adult education known as "hobo colleges" to address the unhealthy working conditions and harsh legal system confronting the working men of the road. After meeting How, Ben had a new goal: to open a hobo college in Chicago.

My father immediately put his own stamp on the new endeavor. In contrast to the humorless missions and other relief agencies of the era, Ben's idea was to "reach the imagination or soul" of the hobo. On his return to Chicago, fired with enthusiasm and boundless energy for the project, Ben recruited social workers, university professors, businessmen, ministers, and labor leaders as speakers. He wrote of the opening of the Chicago Hobo College:

> What an opening Class! Lousy panhandlers, crummy bums, clean sunburned honest stiffs fresh from the wheat fields and resplendent in new overalls, audacious IWW's, cranky communists, derail and canned heat addicts in various stages of alcoholic delirium, jack rollers, fairies and faggots on the make for trade, sticky fingered and slippery tongued punks and petty larceny thieves—not the best looking nor the most intelligent student body, but the strongest smelling class in Chicago.

In addition to his work at the Hobo College, Ben was also involved in organizing and publicizing dinners for the homeless.

During this period, Ben was assisted in his medical practice and in his efforts as a hobo reformer by his laboratory assistant, Grace Amadon. Although he makes few written references to Grace, a brief exchange of letters between her father and Ben speaks volumes. In 1908, Ben received a letter from Grace's father telling him to return the $80 his "hypnotized" daughter had given him through his "unlawful methods . . . making her believe it to be missionary work." According to her father, Grace had borrowed the money and he considered it his duty to repay the lender as fast as possible. The letter was sent by way of the Chicago chief of police.

In his reply Ben acknowledged that Grace had given him money. He went on to say:

> Grace is thirty-six years old. You have always treated her like a child; you have never permitted her to think and reason for herself; you have tried to force upon her an old standard of ethics, morality and religion, in which no educated, scientific person of today believes. . . .
>
> You state that unless I return the money, you will take

some action. I wish you would do it. I am sure the Police Department of Chicago will give you every possible aid, as it would please them immensely to see me in jail.

My father's reply portrays him, at twenty-nine, as a man comfortable with challenging the establishment and confident of his power over women. I can see why Grace, the spinster daughter of such a self-righteous father, would find Ben so exciting and liberating. Grace and Ben would stay in touch for over thirty years. Ben's visit to her at her mother's house when she was in her late sixties suggests she remembered their days together with humor and affection.

Ben often got help with his formal writing. Although the sentiments are surely his, the letter to Grace's father is far too polished for Ben to have written alone. His editor was certainly not Emma Goldman, by then his newest lover. Emma, with Ben's help, would soon be labeled by the press as "the most notorious woman in America." She would have had no time for nonsense like irate fathers.

FIVE

My God, Emma,
How Can You Stand Ben?

The ordinary things that make radicals did not make an
   anarchist of me.
Emma Goldman made me an anarchist.
                        —*From "Following the Monkey," 1925*

My sisters and I knew Emma Goldman as the woman
portrayed in bas relief on her headstone, located near my
father's grave in Chicago's Waldheim Cemetery. As children
we played on the grass by Emma's headstone, and we swung
on the chains and climbed on the marble of the nearby monument to the martyrs of the Haymarket Riot.

My mother told us only that my father and Emma had
worked together teaching people about birth control and
anarchism (without ever explaining the term) and that he and
Emma had been sweethearts long before my mother met him.
He had also been "tarred and feathered" by a vigilante mob
while he was with Emma, she told us. I wasn't clear why, but I
knew that he was very brave to stand up for what he believed
in.

Of all the other women in my father's life, Emma was the
one my mother could have told us most about—had she
cared to. In 1934, when Emma was touring the country, my
mother read her autobiography and attended one of her
lectures in New York. She wrote my father at the time that

Emma's autobiography was "more generous to herself and a little less generous to you, perhaps, than I expected," but that he should "remember the things that the menopause does to a woman."

But by the time my father died, my mother had had more than enough of anarchism and Emma. Her silence to us about Emma could be easily explained by jealousy since my father praised Emma incessantly and sent her Emma's letters despite my mother's protests. But it was Emma's radical politics as well as her constant arguments with my father over who-had-wronged-whom in their long-dead love affair that were more than my mother could tolerate. She hated arguments and was completely apolitical. "Movements such as the labor movement, the birth control movement, the atomic scientists' movement interest me but I remain true to character," she wrote after my father's death. "The only movement I insist on is the daily evacuation."

The passage of time has also given me, and most Americans, a different perspective on Emma than my mother and her generation had when I was growing up. After Emma's death in 1940, "the most notorious woman in America" was remembered primarily in anarchist circles. But with the women's rights movement in the late 1960s, and subsequent research and publications about her, Emma has assumed a more respectable place in American history. With the exception of her banner cause, anarchism, many of the radical ideas for which Emma was despised and persecuted in the early part of the century—organized labor, improved working conditions, free speech, birth control, and equal rights for women—are now central (if still controversial) in American life. Even her stand on draft resistance, for which she was deported in 1919, was an idea supported by a sizable segment of the American population during the Vietnam War.

My father met "Red Emma" Goldman in 1908 when she was thirty-nine, ten years older than he. A fiery orator, she was already established nationally as a champion of anarchy, free speech and free love. Widely read and at ease with European culture, she also spoke on modern literature and drama during her lecture tours. Her career as an anarchist had begun almost twenty years earlier. As a young Russian immigrant working in the clothing sweatshops in Syracuse, New York, Emma had been profoundly affected by the Haymarket Riot in Chicago in 1887. She considered it the cause of her "spiritual birth" to anarchism.

As Emma describes the events in her autobiography, in 1886, workers began calling labor strikes all over the country to bring about the eight-hour work day. During a strike at the McCormick Harvester Company in Chicago, the police attacked a group of strikers, killing several of them. At the mass protest meeting that followed, immigrant anarchists addressed the crowd. The police appeared and began clubbing the crowd to disperse it. In the confusion, someone threw a bomb, wounding and killing a number of policemen.

Because of the local opposition to anarchism, the eight-hour work day, and foreigners, five of these anarchists were sentenced to death; three others were given long-term or life sentences. The last words of August Spies, one of the anarchists sentenced to death, which are commemorated on the Haymarket Monument, were a message my sisters and I read often as children: "The day will come when our silence will be more powerful than the voices you are throttling today."

Emma married a fellow immigrant, Jacob Kershner, but had the courage to leave her unsatisfactory marriage and move to New York City. There she became a political agitator for anarchism and labor rights under the tutelage of the anarchist publisher and speaker, Johann Most. In 1892 Emma aided her comrade lover Alexander (Sasha) Berkman in an attempted assassination of Henry Frick, who had been responsible for violent strikebreaking at the Homestead steel mills in Pennsylvania. Emma and Berkman hoped that Frick's death would be an *Attentat*, a call to action world-wide to right the injustices done to workers by the capitalist owners. But Berkman only wounded Frick. He claimed sole responsibility for the act and was imprisoned for fourteen years. During that time Emma corresponded with him faithfully. She also developed her own philosophy of anarchism and gained increased public visibility as a speaker and labor organizer.

By the time Emma met Ben, Berkman had been out of prison for several years. Though he and Emma were no longer lovers, they continued to live and work together in New York, along with other comrades. Among their activities was the publication of *Mother Earth* magazine and other anarchist literature. Emma also toured the country raising funds for *Mother Earth* and a variety of unpopular political causes.

By 1908, the year of Emma's arrival in Chicago, my father had already acquired a national reputation as a hobo advocate. Following his fledgling start with the Hobo College, and a well-publicized dinner for hoboes, he had begun more serious efforts to collect information on the men of the road, and to speak and write on their behalf. Based on his observations as he tramped across the country, he concluded that his fellow hoboes were not primarily hardened criminals but, instead, young runaways seeking adventure or a better life. These boys and young men, he argued, deserved society's assistance in finding work and a more stable existence.

During the winter of 1907-1908, there was widespread unemployment and labor unrest in Chicago and throughout the country. My father's boldness in leading a march of unemployed men on the Chicago City Hall added to his notoriety. The unrest made the civic authorities in Chicago uneasy. Although Emma was not connected with the event, two days before her arrival in Chicago a young Russian immigrant attempted to assassinate the Chicago chief of police. It was all the police needed to close all meeting halls and keep Emma under close surveillance.

When Ben read in the newspaper that Emma would have no place to speak, he contacted her host, a former medical school classmate of his, to offer the Hobo College for a hall. He also notified the newspapers that Emma would be speaking there. A reporter contacted the police, and the fire marshal immediately closed the hall to crowds.

Ben went to meet Emma with the bad news. Twenty years later, both of them remembered that meeting vividly. Ben recalled, "She had a powerful face, beautiful, strong, clear blue eyes, a nose that was not Jewish, and a strong, firm jaw. She was somewhat nearsighted and wore heavy glasses. Her hair was blond and silken and she wore it in a simple knot on the back of her head."

Emma's description was much more evocative of her feelings:

> My visitor was a tall man with a finely shaped head, covered by a mass of black curly hair, which had evidently not been washed for some time. His eyes were brown, large and dreamy. His lips, disclosing beautiful teeth when he smiled, were full and passionate. He looked a handsome brute. His hands, narrow and white, exerted a particular fascination. His fingernails, like his hair, seemed to be on strike against soap and brush. I could not take my eyes off his hands. A strange charm seemed to emanate from them, caressing and stirring.

Emma was not able to speak in Chicago, but Ben went to hear her in Minneapolis. "She had the voice of the Angel Gabriel," he later recalled. "It was a clarion call for the people to rise and bethink themselves. It was an appeal to humanity to organize, to educate, to emancipate, to throw off tyranny, exploitation and ignorance. Friend and foe knew her power on the lecture platform." Without being asked, Ben took charge of the pamphlet sales in the back of the room.

They became lovers on their return to Chicago. Later Emma wrote, "That night . . . I was caught in the torrent of elemental passion I had never dreamed any man could rouse in me. I responded shamelessly to its primitive call, its naked beauty, its ecstatic joy."

Emma was brought back to reality the following evening when she saw Ben exchange pleasantries with a police captain in the restaurant where she and her friends were having dinner. She left without speaking to him. After Ben begged in letters and telegrams for a chance to explain, Emma had a dream about him. "Flames were shooting from his fingertips and slowly enveloping my body," she recalled. "I made no attempt to escape them. I strained toward them, craving to be consumed by their fire." She decided she could inspire Ben to work in the world of her "social ideals" and wired him: "Come."

When they met, Emma accepted Ben's explanation that he was friendly with the police because he frequently pleaded for the hoboes with the authorities. He offered to pay his own fare if he could be with her, and Emma agreed to take him on tour as her manager. They left for California in spite of Emma's misgivings about what her comrades would think of Ben. "I resolved to have him," she wrote later. "Let the rest take care of itself."

Thanks to Ben's untiring efforts, their first trip was immensely successful and a forerunner of tours to come. Emma had always depended on local comrades to arrange for halls and to handle publicity. With Ben's flair for the dramatic and shocking, and his skill at providing good copy for newspaper editors, Emma drew thousands in the larger cities. More importantly, these new audiences came from middle-class America, a public Emma had not attracted earlier.

Ben also excelled at working a crowd for pamphlet and book sales. He recalled his sales pitch for Ibsen's *The Doll's*

House at Emma's talk on modern drama:

> I have another little pamphlet here, friends. . . . It's about a
> woman named Nora. Nora got tired of living with her
> husband and taking care of the kids. One day she said to her
> old man, "You are just like the rest of men, always trying to
> boss me and never giving me an even break. I am going to
> get the hell out of here and leave you to take care of the
> kids." Now, if there is anybody in this audience who wishes
> his wife to leave him let him take this pamphlet home and
> give it to her. Who'll be the next? Thank you. I have only six
> more of these left, friends.

Ben added that, in the ten years he was with Emma, "we
sold more books and works of literature than any other two
propagandists in the United States . . . The publisher of
Whitman's *Leaves of Grass* told me that for several years Emma
was his best customer." Pamphlet sales were equally good.
What I Believe sold more than 50,000 copies. *Love and
Marriage* and *The Tragedy of Woman's Emancipation* also did
well. "The ordinary listener . . . would take one of her
pamphlets even if he had to walk home," Ben recalled.

Ben found the clashes with the police exciting. Years later
he wrote to a friend, "Before Emma Goldman, most of my
crimes were vagrancy, riding on freight trains without permission and panhandling. With Emma Goldman I was often
arrested, charged with anarchy, denouncing the government
as unnecessary, speaking without a permit, and conspiracy to
destroy the government." In time, "preaching birth control"
was added to the list, and my father drew a harsher sentence
for that offense than anyone else in America.

Ben also enjoyed the writers, labor agitators, and radicals
he met through Emma. However, he was hardly the ideal
companion. His deliberate efforts to shock people made
Emma uneasy. Ben's idea of an icebreaker at a dinner party

was to loudly ask a strange woman, "Sister, how old was the baby before you got married?" When one embarrassed woman asked her husband, "Sam, why did you tell him that?" the husband punched Ben in the jaw.

To make Ben more acceptable, Emma tried to educate him through their conversations and the books she read to him on their long train rides. Later he wrote:

> Much that I know about the world and life I learned from Emma or at her guidance. The significance of history, the meaning of literature and the beauty of art all came to me while I nestled securely under the tutelage of Emma. . . . She picked me up an intellectual ragamuffin and a bankrupt social reformer, and to use her own terms, she made me a "playboy of the western world," intellectually and socially solvent.

I'm sure Emma's tutoring had a major effect on my father, but she was not so satisfied with her pupil's progress as he was, particularly years later.

However, no one would dispute that their passionate relationship fueled the productivity of their work. Emma described Ben as the one man she had met "who would love the woman in me and yet who would be able to share my work. . . . Ben had come when I had greatest need of him." Ben called the years with Emma "the most emphatic chapter in my life." What Emma did not know on the first tour, however, was that she was not Ben's only lover. From the beginning, he found women—sometimes at her lectures—for casual sexual encounters.

When the first tour was over, Emma returned to Berkman and her other comrades in New York, and Ben returned to Chicago to see his mother.

Emma's fears about Ben's acceptability were realized after he rejoined her in New York. Ben did not fit in with her intellectual, primarily European comrades at the *Mother Earth* headquarters. Berkman, in particular, distrusted and criticized Ben and even wrote for confirmation of his medical degree. Late in life my father recalled his reception by Emma's friends to Leonard Abbott, a former comrade of Emma and Ben's:

> Voltairine de Cleyre used to say to Emma Goldman, "My God, Emma, how can you stand Ben?" Most of Emma's friends agreed with you that I was the most vulgar and impossible man they'd ever met. . . . Emma Goldman dwelt on the fact. There have been so many people like you, alternately disgusted with me, and then attracted to me. . . . But I never meant to be disgusting to you or anybody else.

This ability to intensely attract people and then repel them by his behavior would stay with my father throughout his life.

While he was in New York, Ben spent much of his time in Greenwich Village, where his open pursuit of sex was acceptable to its bohemian residents. In contrast, the more serious anarchists found that aspect of his behavior offensive, not only then but years later. Near the end of my father's life, Abbott wrote to him, "You are too ready to assume that every man wants to copulate with every woman he meets and vice versa. You do not sufficiently differentiate between sacred and profane love." Ben agreed.

Ben's unhappiness around Emma's friends led her to consider a tour out of the country. She decided to put Berkman in charge of *Mother Earth* and leave for Australia with Ben at the end of their second American tour.

What prompted my father's next move is unclear. Perhaps he was testing Emma to see how outrageous he could be. Perhaps he was caught in one of his impulsive changes of heart. In any case, according to Emma's autobiography, a few days before he was to leave to do the advance publicity, Ben wrote her a long letter. The letter explained that he had been the one who informed a reporter she would be speaking at the Hobo College in Chicago, and that the reporter had notified the police; that he had borrowed money to pay for his fare on the first tour and was gradually paying it back from the litera- ture sales receipts; and that he was also supporting his mother from the same money. He also confessed that he had had numerous lovers on the tour, including women whose names he did not even know. "I sat numb," Emma remembered. "The terrible letter seemed to creep over me, word by word, and drawing me into its slime."

After the publication of Emma's autobiography in 1931, Ben offered his own version of their early financial arrangements:

> If Emma Goldman could live and work with me for ten years and then intimate that I was a thief because out of the tens of thousands of dollars we earned together, I sent a few dollars to my mother while Emma sent thousands of dollars to Berkman and other comrades I have no objections.

Whatever the truth of their finances, the most difficult problem for Emma was Ben's infidelity. She wrote:

> I have propagated freedom in sex. I have had many men myself. But I loved them. . . . It will be painful, lacerating to feel myself one of many in Ben's life. It will be a fearful price to pay for my love. But nothing worth while is gained except at heavy cost. I've paid dearly for the right to myself, for my social ideal, for everything I have achieved. Is my love for him so weak that I shall not be able to pay the price his freedom of action demands?

In her autobiography written twenty years later, Emma stated that being with Ben was worth the pain, and that she accepted the person that he was. According to her current biographers, however, Emma's letters to Ben at the time reveal that she was tormented by Ben's relationships with other women for the rest of their years together. This conflict between the public Emma Goldman who lectured on free love, and the private woman who doubted her work because she was tortured by Ben's infidelity is, for me, one of the most fascinating aspects of Emma's life.

Why Emma chose to return to my father again and again over nine years is clear from their passionate correspondence that neither would repeat with other lovers. Treasure box (t-b) became the code words for Emma's vagina, mountains (m) for her breasts, willie (w) for Ben's penis. Sample exchanges include:

> Emma: Please, please write me every day and tell me you love me. Tell me that you want the t-b and m. You don't know what you are missing Hobo dear. The m. are tremendous, always keeping their heads erect on guard for Hobo. The t-b is full of red wine and wails for w- to drink it all. . . .
>
> You are like Anarchism to me. The more I struggle for it the further it grows away from me. The more I struggle for your love, your devotion, the further away it seems from me. Yet struggle I must. For like liberty, you are the highest Goal to me, the most precious treasure.

> Ben: I hold you close. I bite you and pledge you that I want to and will try so hard in my own fool way to make you happy. . . . Tell the mountains to look out for Hobo is going to eat them and tell the dear treasure box to prepare for great floods.

Despite her turmoil, Emma and Ben started on their tour. But when they reached California, they heard that Emma's estranged husband's citizenship had been revoked. Since Emma was no longer a citizen, if she left the country she would not be readmitted. They canceled their Australian tour, and returned to New York where she began work on publishing some of her lectures.

When Emma was unable to find a publisher, it was Ben who encouraged her to publish the book herself. Long used to living on borrowed money, he predicted they could pay back the loan for the printing from sales on the next tour. Apparently Emma did not object in this case. Berkman edited and proofread the manuscript and *Anarchism and Other Essays* came off the press in time for the next tour in 1912.

Along with Bill Haywood and Elizabeth Gurley Flynn, Emma and Ben strongly supported the activities of the IWW (Industrial Workers of the World), a labor group that encompassed striking textile-mill workers in the East and migratory workers in the West. Their tour included San Diego, a city where IWW members, or "Wobblies," had been subjected to extreme harassment, including capture and torture, by a group of vigilantes. Emma and Ben arrived in Los Angeles in time for a public demonstration to protest the killing of Joseph Mikolasek, an IWW "soapboxer," by the police in his San Diego home.

On the evening Ben and Emma arrived in San Diego, Emma was decoyed into leaving their hotel room. Armed men then entered the room and forced Ben to drive out into the desert with them. In the glare of car headlights, the men stripped Ben, beat and kicked him severely, poured tar on him, and lacking feathers, rubbed sagebrush in the tar. For good measure, they burned "IWW" on his buttocks with a lit cigar. They weren't done. As Ben later described it, "One very gentle businessman who is active in church work very deliberately attempted to push my cane into my rectum. One unassuming banker twisted my testicles."

The vigilantes left Ben his vest with his money, railroad ticket and watch, as well as his underwear, afraid, Ben thought, that he would meet some women. After they left, he stumbled back to a small town where he was able to buy some clothes and turpentine. He walked on to Escondido, tele-graphed Emma, and caught the next train to Los Angeles.

Emma had left San Diego for Los Angeles after Ben's capture, fearful that he might be killed. She recalled later when the train pulled into Los Angeles, "Ben lay in a rear car, all huddled up. He was in blue overalls, his face deathly pale, a terrified look in his eyes. . . . At the sight of me he cried: 'Oh, Mommy, I'm with you at last! Take me away, take me home!'"

Whether my father's statements were as dramatic as Emma remembered, there's no question he was terrified by the experience. Compounding the unpopularity of the IWW cause, on the day before Ben and Emma's arrival, a San Diego newspaper had run a story about my father's abandonment of May Reitman and his baby daughter in 1902. I'm sure he considered himself lucky to have escaped the vigilantes with his life.

Whatever his feelings were while he lay in the baggage car, it did not take my father long to recover. In his later years he would entertain his friends with the story of the protest meeting that followed. The large crowd of radicals in Los Angeles was in a sober mood after hearing Emma and the other speakers. But Ben's speech, full of humorous sugges-tions about showing the scars on his buttocks, if only there were no ladies present, left the crowd laughing.

Not everyone was amused, however. An editorial in the May 19, 1912, edition of the *Los Angeles Times* read:

> The *Times* does not commend the fowl[sic] treatment accorded by the San Diegans to the anarchist doctor, but it does not attempt to sit in judgment on those who discour-aged his longer stay. . . . Maybe he got, on the whole, what was coming to him.

Socialist Eugene Debs disagreed: "The cannibals who tarred and darkened Ben Reitman in the name of 'law and order' are below the level of a tribe of head hunters . . . and a time will come when their children will blush with shame to hear their names."

SIX

I Am Always Behind
Some Group, Some Woman

Of course the fact that there was plenty of travel, excitement, probably held me a little longer in the anarchist
movement than it would have in a Christian Science
church.

—From "Following the Monkey," 1925

San Diego was a turning point for my father and Emma. "I
left San Diego a beaten man and could not get it out of my
mind," he wrote. He insisted they return the following year.
His opportunity to test his courage came quickly. Emma and
Ben were arrested shortly after stepping off the train, and
jailed for safety from the rabid vigilante mob until they could
be escorted to the next train. After their terrifying and humiliating experience with the vigilantes, Emma would never let
my father forget she thought him a coward, particularly in
comparison to Berkman.

When Emma and Ben returned to New York in 1913, Ben
encouraged Emma to find larger living quarters so he could
invite his mother to live with them. When Ida Reitman
arrived, the rift between Emma and Ben that had begun in
San Diego widened. Brave as she was with repressive police
and angry mobs, Emma was no match for my grandmother.
Emma wrote twenty years later:

I understood her very well: she was one of the millions

whose minds had been stunted by the limitations of their lives. Her approval or disapproval would have mattered little to me if it had not been that Ben was as madly obsessed by his mother as she with him. . . . She was constantly on his mind, his passion for her a menace to his love for any other woman.

Emma's own maternal feelings towards Ben have drawn comments from biographers and book critics. Ben often referred to Emma as "Mommy" and she called him "Hobo" or "my boy." In her autobiography, Emma was apologetic about their age difference, but Ben did not think it was a barrier between them. "Emma at fifty surpassed any woman I ever knew at twenty-five. She not only had an intellectual development and spiritual security that was greater than any other time in her life, but she had a physical capacity for work and love."

Emma's attempts at generosity toward Ida were never enough and the quarrels between Emma and Ben intensified until Emma threw a chair at him and told Ben and his mother to leave. Ben and Ida moved into an apartment for a brief period and then returned to Chicago. In Ben's absence, Emma began a series of lectures which became the nucleus for her second book, *The Social Significance of Modern Drama*.

After a two-month separation and innumerable letters, Emma and Ben were reunited. Emma explained why in her autobiography:

I began to realize the wisdom of the Russian peasant saying: "If you drink, you'll die, and if you don't drink, you'll die. Better drink and die." To be away from Ben meant sleepless nights, restless days, sickening yearning. To be near him involved conflict and strife, daily denial of my pride, but it also meant ecstasy and renewed vigor for my work. . . . If the price was high, I would pay it; but I would drink, I would drink!

Their next major campaign was birth control. Although Margaret Sanger, who coined the term, is generally credited as the person behind this country's birth control movement, it was a radical cause in America long before Sanger. In the late 1800s, Moses Harman, a free lover and anarchist from Kansas, served several jail terms for distributing birth control literature.

Emma began speaking on the topic in a general way after 1900. However, to avoid risking arrest under the Comstock laws, she did not give out specific methods at her lectures. Ben and Emma claimed that Margaret Sanger first got involved with the birth control issue after attending Emma's lectures. Once Sanger dissociated herself from the radicals and focused on the single topic of birth control, she grew increasingly effective as an organizer and educator.

In 1937 my father wrote to Norman Himes, the author of the first history of contraception, about his failure to acknowledge the contribution by the radicals to the birth control movement:

Moses Harman
Was the true father of American Birth Control. . . .

I mean your prejudice against the RADICALS
Is so great that you COULD not give them credit.
Emma Goldman
More than any one person in America
Popularized B. C.
She was Margaret Sanger's INSPIRATION
No that ain't the word
Margaret imitated and denied her.
Emma was the first person in America
To lecture on Birth Control
    in one hundred cities. . . .
The physicians, social scientists, clergy & etc.
Became interested in B.C.

Only after the Radicals had "broken" the ground.
And gone to jail.

Ben had generally remained in the background while Emma was on the lecture platform. But now, with the advent of their birth control campaign, he was in his element. Both he and Emma lectured on birth control and other sexual topics. Ben's contribution to the campaign also included the publication of an anonymous pamphlet *Why and How the Poor Should Not Have Children.* Based on the pioneering work of Dr. William Robinson, it described the use of the condom, diaphragm, chemically treated cotton ball (the forerunner of the cervical sponge) and douches. What children routinely learn in school today was groundbreaking and shocking in 1913. "Children do not need to be born by accident," my father boldly wrote in his pamphlet. "It is not wicked or dangerous to use methods for the prevention of conception. Many people use preventatives for years until they are able to support a child; and then they have one." Rather than risk arrest, Emma and Ben continued to avoid speaking openly about birth control methodology. Instead, they gave this pamphlet away free.

It was Margaret Sanger's pamphlet *Family Limitations* that brought Emma to a turning point. Sanger's activities in New York had been closely watched by Anthony Comstock and the New York Society for the Suppression of Vice. In 1915, after the arrest of Sanger's husband for handing a copy of her pamphlet to a Comstock agent, Emma decided to support the Sangers' work. "The time had come when I must either stop lecturing on the subject or do it practical justice," she wrote. "I felt I must share with them the consequences of the birth control issue." She decided to include a more explicit talk on birth control in her eighth tour with Ben. In addition to birth control, her lectures that year included "anti-war topics, the fight for Caplin and Schmidt [accused of bombing the *Los*

Angeles Times building], freedom in love, and the problem most tabooed in polite society, homosexuality."

Emma's first arrest for distributing birth control literature came in the spring of 1916. Sentenced to a fine of $100 or fifteen days in the workhouse, she chose jail. At a protest meeting on her behalf, Ben encouraged the audience to take the free birth control pamphlets. He was arrested and sentenced to sixty days in the workhouse. While Ben was serving his sentence, Emma decided to leave on the next tour without him because "his letters breathed a serenity I had never known him to feel before." Emma would soon learn the cause for his mood. While Ben was in prison, he was seriously considering leaving Emma for a younger anarchist he had fallen in love with, Anna Martindale.

Ben joined Emma after his release but they began arguing immediately. For the first time Ben spoke openly about wanting to start a family with Anna. Emma reminded him pitifully, "You have a child, your little Helen! Have you ever shown paternal love for her, or even the least interest?" But she could not change Ben's mind.

Emma and Ben separated for a month, but Ben returned to finish their tour. He was arrested in Cleveland, Ohio, and in Rochester, New York for distributing birth control literature. Ben later described his dealings with the police and judges: "they have always given me a fair deal, Judge Cull in Cleveland being the only exception." Although he was acquitted in Rochester, Cleveland was a different story: a delayed sentence of six months in the workhouse and a $1,000 fine, the heaviest sentence ever given for the offense of distributing birth control propaganda in this country.

When the United States entered the First World War in 1917, Emma and Ben began a battle even more dangerous than birth control. Following the presidential signing of the draft bill, Emma and her comrades immediately began organizing opposition to the draft with the No-Conscription

League. She wrote passionately against the draft: "Free-born Americans had to be forcibly pressed into the military mold, herded like cattle, and shipped across the waters to fertilize the fields of France." Along with Emma and her comrades, Ben began to give antiwar and antidraft speeches and to write similar articles for *Mother Earth.*

Emma's and Ben's autobiographies disagree on what happened next. Emma recalled that at the height of the antiwar campaign, Ben decided to join Anna, who was by then pregnant and waiting for him in Chicago. Emma saw no need for Ben to leave. She wrote, "The young woman of his Sunday class . . . was neither in danger nor in want, and her child was not expected for months to come." Shortly after Ben's departure, Emma and Berkman were arrested in the *Mother Earth* office for conspiracy against the draft and their files were confiscated. Despite this crisis, Ben did not return.

Ben recalled that he left after their imprisonment and the movement collapsed. In either case, Ben left Emma for a completely different way of life with Anna.

Emma and Berkman were sentenced to two years each in prison and a $10,000 fine. Only Emma's secretary, Fitzi, remained to hold the "tattered and scattered ends of the Anarchist, Anti-militarist and Birth Control propaganda" together.

In his autobiography, my father wondered why Emma and Berkman had been singled out for such harsh treatment when he was never even arrested for his antiwar propaganda. He suggested that his friendliness with the police may have helped, but a more significant factor was the public attitude that "the opponents of war were the foreign radicals . . . who knew no better than to bite the hand that was feeding them." An American-born physician, he escaped temporarily.

My father also wrestled over the reasons why he left Emma and the anarchist movement. Was it "to save his miserable hide" when others were being arrested and possibly shot?

He offered other reasons: his love for Anna, his need for a child, and the growing antagonism he felt from Berkman and the other comrades. Originally, Emma's comrades looked upon him as "a novelty, a boy, a janitor, a clown and a necessary evil. But, as I began to develop a soul of my own and showed a faint spark of intelligence and was beginning to be a power and an influence, I felt a real or imaginary increase in opposition."

He concluded that the most significant reason for his abandoning anarchism and the antiwar work was he was no longer in love with Emma. He wrote, "I feel certain that, had Emma Goldman been a Socialist, a Theosophist, a Buddhist, a pure food crank, or a single taxer, I should have joined her party with the same zeal and enthusiasm that I brought to the anarchist movement."

While my father would fall in and out of love many times during the remainder of his life, I believe he left Emma and the anarchist movement because, basically, it was too confining. For all the exhilaration he felt from the idea of making history with Emma, the price he paid was living in her shadow. Although in later life he would often attempt to capitalize on their relationship, the image of himself as Emma's "janitor" would haunt him long after he had gone on to many other roles. He wrote a friend years later: "In the RED NETWORK, a who's who and hand-book of Radicals, there is a list of all dangerous radicals. Under Ben Reitman it reads 'See Free Society Groups, also Emma Goldman.' That is very well put. I am always behind some group, some woman."

But for then, he appeared to have put the group and the woman behind him. He recalled the train ride back to Chicago:

I felt the solemnity of the occasion. The habits, the friendships, the loves of the past ten years and a consciousness that I had left the propaganda when my comrades really needed me—all these things produced feelings of pain, regret, hope, joy, and uncertainty. . . . A loving Mother, a loving wife, a devoted brother and a big automobile met me and drove us to my first real home in Chicago.

SEVEN

A Free and Glorious Mother

Business was good. I was getting along well at the Health Department. The Dill Pickle and the Hobo College flourished. The world looked rosy and the future had tremendous possibilities.

—*From "Following the Monkey," 1925*

As a child, all I knew about Anna Martindale was that she was our father's second wife and our half-brother Brutus's mother. She had died before my mother met my father, my mother told us. After Anna's death, my father kept her ashes in an urn in his apartment.

In contrast to her silence about Anna, my mother spoke willingly of Brutus. Our big brother was a wonderful young man who enjoyed his little sisters, she told us often. He would have taken care of us had he not died so young. In trying to recall my feelings of what was missing in my childhood, it was not a father, but a big brother to look after me. Among the few mementos from my childhood is the picture of Brutus my mother gave me.

When I first began searching for Anna's story, I found information sparse. Relatives recall her as a quiet, sweet woman, a pleasant hostess, "very English," and long-suffering about Ben's affairs with other women. In contrast to his dramatic portrait of Emma, my father's description of Anna in "Following the Monkey" is a thinly drawn picture of the mother of his son and the loving wife who supported his work as a physician and reformer. In later letters, my father wrote that her support of him had contributed to her death. "I eat her up," was his expression. Recent publications have added some detail, while leaving much missing. But the more pieces of the puzzle of Anna I discover, the stronger her personality becomes. Passive women, like Ben's first wife May, did not last long around my father.

Anna was born in 1884 in the mill town of Bradford, England, to a poor Jewish family. According to Rev. Frank Beck, Ben's colleague and close friend, her father would not or could not work, which she greatly resented. From the time she was a young girl, she and her mother, sister, and two brothers "worked like hell for a paltry wage in the sweatshop and the mill."

As she grew older, Anna advanced from unskilled child labor in a hosiery mill to a skilled trade as a dressmaker. Inhumane working conditions brought her into the labor movement. After immigrating to America in 1911 or 1912, she continued her labor activities in New York as a member of the Women's Trade Union League. After hearing Emma Goldman speak, she was strongly attracted to the anarchist's philosophy.

Ben met Anna in 1912 when she came into the *Mother Earth* office to buy anarchist literature. The tall, attractive, blue-eyed blond woman was then twenty-eight—five years younger than he and fifteen years younger than Emma. Ben and Anna soon became lovers.

In the summer of 1912, Emma wrote Ben a letter, accusing him once again of infidelity, and listing his current female correspondents. In his denial to Emma, ("I want no one but you") Ben explained each of the women in turn. "As to Anna," he wrote, "she is my mother's friend and never meant any-thing to me despite what her letter may convey." He ended the letter to Emma, "Baby I is going to be good and faithful and save stamps."

Anna shared Emma's commitment to anarchy and free love, but otherwise they were opposites. A woman of action—articulate, critical, and controlling—Emma was the dominant force in her relationship with Ben. Anna was artistic, inarticulate—often to the point of silence—and strongly supportive of Ben and his work. In this relationship Ben was the dominant partner. Unlike Emma, who enjoyed sex for its own sake and never wanted children, the reserved Anna felt that a child was the highest form of love between a man and a woman. Most significantly, Anna knew from the beginning she was one of the many "other women" to Emma.

By 1916 Ben was seriously considering alternatives to life with Emma. "I had always thought of Chicago as my home and the one place I could rest. I began to dream of a home with my mother, my wife and baby and a steady practice. I had visions of myself teaching in a medical college, of being an active reformer to the outcasts and an active worker in the church." Anna's letters and loving support during Ben's two-month imprisonment at Blackwell's Island convinced him that she was the right person for his new life. He wrote in his autobiography, "When I was released from the Long Island Prison in July, 1916, Anna Martindale and I decided to be united as soon as possible."

Ben was more circumspect in his writings about Anna while they were living together than he would be later. Although he always referred to her as his wife, he and Anna were never legally married. Not only was Anna a freelover by choice, she was a woman ready to have Ben's child. Even though Ben was still living and working with Emma in New York part of the time, Anna moved to Chicago to be with him in 1916 and became pregnant the following year. She must have recognized that Ben might not leave Emma, yet was willing to take her chances.

Anna also knew the kind of life she wanted. In contrast to Emma's small apartment where the *Mother Earth* office also functioned as the sitting room and bedroom, Anna selected and furnished an apartment in an imposing building on Chicago's Gold Coast. Ben was surprised on his return from his "final" break with Emma. "The house was artistically decorated and comfortably furnished," he wrote. "It took me quite a while to become acclimated; it was hard for me to really feel I had a wife and home of my own—but it was just what I wanted."

By Ben's account, when they started life together, Anna had a few hundred dollars saved, but he had nothing to contribute from his years with Emma. His only financial resource was $500 that had been given him by an anarchist comrade, Agnes Inglis, towards his $1,000 fine in Cleveland, then under appeal.

The beginning of my father's private practice typified much of his later medical career. Unconcerned about income, and attracted to Chicago's underserved populations, he opened his office for business. He wrote later:

> From the very first day I opened my office, I had a few patients and a great many visiting friends. My office was just a few blocks from Bughouse Square, in the center of Hobohemia, near to many labor union headquarters, across the street from the Chicago Avenue Police Station, and near the County Jail. I was in the center of a modest vice area—gamblers, prostitutes and pool-halls all around me.

In order to make a living for his new family, Ben again called on his former mentor from medical school, John Dill Robertson, by then the commissioner of the Chicago Board of Health. Despite opposition to Ben's work as an anarchist from a number of "patriotic, social service and medical organizations," Robertson remained supportive. He hired Ben for a part-time public health position doing smallpox vaccinations in the black and hobo districts of Chicago.

Venereal disease was my father's special interest almost from the beginning. The First World War had focused increased medical attention on venereal disease as a serious public health problem. Over thirteen percent of American servicemen were found to be infected, most having been infected during civilian life. Like other major city public health departments, the Chicago Health Department began an active venereal disease campaign. Ben suggested to Robertson that the time was right to establish a municipal venereal disease clinic. Ben also had the support of Dr. William Evans, one of Ben's mentors at the Polyclinic and Chicago's previous health commissioner. Robertson appointed Ben as one of the first three physicians staffing the new clinic.

Ben's new duties were in sharp contrast to treatment at today's often crowded and austere public health facilities. "The clinic hours were social hours," he remembered. "We not only gave them Salvarsan [a drug for syphilis], but [Dr.] Will Pennington used to sing to them. And doctors and patients often sat and discussed life and love and the pursuit of women."

Ben also resumed his activities on behalf of hobo welfare, often speaking at the Hobo College or recruiting other speakers. His greatest joy, however, was his role as unofficial chairman and press agent for the Dill Pickle Club.

By 1916 the Dill Pickle had been around for several years as a small radical coffeehouse. It became a Chicago landmark when its founder, Jack Jones, moved the club to larger quarters in Tooker Alley on Chicago's Near North Side. Over the next ten years, the format of the club attracted Chicago's famous literary figures—Carl Sandburg, Sherwood Anderson, Edgar Lee Masters, and Vachel Lindsey—along with a collection of artists, playwrights, feminists, radicals, and onlookers.

With Ben's skills as a press agent, "Sunday night meetings were Monday morning news." An important element of the forum was the heckling from the audience. "No matter how rotten the speakers were, a joint committee of 'razzers' was on hand to make the meeting thrilling and joyful."

Ben's family life was also a source of satisfaction. Sixteen years after the birth of the daughter that he abandoned, he was now ready for fatherhood. He wrote of the birth of his son Benjamin, nicknamed Brutus, in February 1918, "I don't know of anything more glorious or spiritual than to kneel beside the woman you love, and hold in your arms a child of love and desire." His euphoria did not last long, however. One month later he received a telegram to report immediately to Cleveland to begin his six-month sentence and pay his $1,000 fine. Without money to pay the fine, there was a possibility his sentence could be extended up to five years.

By this time, Emma already had been a prisoner for a full year. Ben visited once, early in her sentence, but it was a painful experience.

> It was strange to see my little blue-eyed "Mommy" in prison garb, with the pain of compulsory confinement and forced labor written on her face. We could not say the things we felt, hostile eyes were on us. Emma and I were conscious of "my desertion to her and the cause." It was a painful visit. I had a cheap way of comforting myself. I was able to buy her a few dollars worth of food.

Emma was back where she had begun—in the sweatshop—this time in the prison clothing factory. Although her incoming and outgoing mail was read by prison authorities, she was able to maintain communication with her friends and comrades. Emma found that letters from Ben, "breathing the old assurance of his love, were like coals of fire."

Ben's letters describing his approaching fatherhood were particularly distressing for Emma. "Whether it was the defeat of my own motherhood or the pain that another should have given Ben what I would not, his rhapsodies increased my resentment against him and everyone connected with him." This resentment stayed with her. She never mentioned Anna by name in her autobiography.

When Ben surrendered to the prison authorities in Warrensville, Ohio, he was assigned to a prison farm and county facilities complex. In contrast to Emma and, particularly, Alexander Berkman, who spent long periods of time in solitary confinement, Ben was given unusual freedom. Moreover, my father could make even jail seem a joyful experience. He wrote later:

> Jail was always a delightful place to me. I learned much while there. It was the only place in life where I kept regular hours. Oh the profitable hours I spent listening to real criminals tell of their activities. "They told me all the safes they cracked, and all the lies they ever knew."

Assigned as an assistant physician to the medical director, Ben moved freely between buildings to treat the patients in the jail, insane asylum, poorhouse, and tuberculosis hospital. In those days before antibiotics, and in the primitive conditions of the prison, he often could do little for the seriously ill patients. He wrote to Anna in 1918:

> To see men suffer and die and not be able to help is terrible, but I am able to ease their pain a little and it's so easy to be kind. Wilde said, "And never a human voice comes near to speak a gentle word." I am learning to be gentle and brutal. I needed this jail experience and I feel they need me here.

In addition to his work and correspondence, Ben found

time to begin the "Outcast Narratives," his unpublished collection of poetry. Over the years, his observations of his patients, his radical and bohemian friends, and the men he had known on the road became the material for his free verse.

In a self-portrait, he wrote of his isolation from his former anarchist comrades, and his hope that he had gotten the best of the bargain:

Ben

Ben used to be an agitator.
Spent ten years in active propaganda.
Then he stopped it and settled down.
Got married and had a child.
His comrades called him "deserter and coward."

He tried to explain himself in the following:

You call me a coward and deserter.
You say "It is too bad, but it is true.
What could you expect? He is only a Christian."
Only a Christian with a Jew's love for children,
An Anarchist's passion for freedom,
And an ordinary man's desire for a wife and a home. . . .

But I got the best of you all.
A thousand voices may sing your praises,
Countries pay you just homage,
Nations fight for possession of you,
Posterity proclaim you saviors and heroes,
But I shall have a child that loves me.

A child born in the greatest age,
Of a free and glorious mother,
A child who is welcome,

And who will fulfill all the unfulfilled
Hopes of his father.
To rid the world of wars, poverty and diseases.

Only one letter/poem from Anna to Ben in prison has been found, but it documents her idealism:

The starting of the little life with health of mind and body
Sound in inner and outer sight and sense;

And with companionship, care, guidance
Devotion, provision through the years—sacrifice fulfillment:

God! To be a great Mother fully creative
With you a great father:

Perhaps I would not care if you had not known the depths,
If I had not known

You have taken upon yourself
"The sins of the world"
In overcoming them there shall come to you
Untold riches of the Spirit and—Fatherhood.

Whatever "riches of the Spirit" my father might have found in prison, he also found the flesh easy to satisfy there. Towards the end of his life, he shed his reticence about discussing one phase of prison life in a letter to his friend Theodore Schroeder, who was gathering material to write Ben's biography:

I got a lot of love in jail and plenty of sex. You'll pardon my French but I jazzed the female prisoners and some of the female guards and not a few of the female visitors. And if nobody's looking, I can tell you I enjoyed a few of the male homosexuals. Yes I took my fun where I found it and denied myself nothing.

During his stay at Warrensville, Ben wrote to Emma and asked her help in raising money for his fine so he would be freed at the end of his six-month term. Still in prison, Emma tried to solicit the remaining money from friends. She was furious when she learned from a friend that Ben's fine had been reduced to $500 since she knew he had been given that amount by their mutual friend Agnes Inglis. What Emma did not know was that Ben still needed the money. Agnes's contribution had been used to support Anna and the baby in his absence.

Fortunately, Ben had other resources. Rose Siegel, a schoolteacher in New York, who had been Ben's occasional lover since his earliest days with Emma, gave him the needed money. Ben remained grateful to Rose. Upon his release from prison, he "disappointed his wife a little by staying over in Toledo a day", presumably with Rose, and later married her after Anna's death.

Other women also aided Ben while he was in prison. Sadie (Sarah) Watchmaker, a mentally unstable woman, gave Ben $30 and a watch. She later hired a lawyer to get her money and watch back and claimed that "she was lovesick and hypnotized" by him. Sarah remained doggedly devoted to Ben for almost fifteen years. Ben took her gifts when she had money. He also returned both sympathy and handouts when she fell on hard times in the worst of the Depression.

In his autobiography, Ben recalled that on the train from Cleveland to Chicago, "I read my Bible, and prayed that God would give me an opportunity to serve my fellow-man and to let me do some more work in jail." The day after his return to Chicago he opened his practice in his, then vacant, old office. Between the flu epidemic and the war effort, physicians were scarce in Chicago. Ben was rehired by the Chicago Health

Department and Dr. Robertson assigned him to the newly formed venereal disease clinic in the Chicago House of Correction. Later, he also was involved in starting a venereal disease clinic at the Cook County Jail.

My father's work in the Chicago jails was an expansion of his lifetime specialization in venereal disease. He wrote that during his first two years in the jail clinic, he "treated thousands of men and women for syphilis and gonorrhea on a wholesale scale, with a recklessness, a daring, and a rapidity that would frighten the average V.D. specialist." He trained prisoners to be his orderlies, bragging that he could make a better nurse in two weeks than the county hospital could in three years.

Ben also boasted that he never had any fatalities, "but I came very near to it many times"—not surprising since the treatment for syphilis in those days utilized highly toxic metal compounds.

One day I was shooting Salvarsan at the rate of "one a minute." This included the time the patient got on and off the table. Someone called my attention to the fact that one of the patients to whom I had just given an intravenous injection of neo-Salvarsan, had fallen on the floor. I turned around and discovered that the last five patients I had injected were lying on the floor gasping for breath. We stopped for about five minutes, resuscitated the patients; and then went right on with the work.

My father's warmth towards his prisoner patients, and his willingness to listen to them, brought private patients to his growing venereal disease practice. Male convicts and ex-convicts also recommended him to their lovers and wives. His sympathetic treatment of the homosexual prisoners, usually abused and humiliated by the authorities and other prisoners, brought him more patients from this group. This is not to imply that my father was consistently sympathetic to homosexuals throughout his career—my father wasn't consistently anything. His papers describe both his own homosexual experiences and his verbal abuse of a group of homosexuals while on a bus in the early 1930s.

Emma was still in prison, but with increasing governmental repression of alien anarchists, her stay in America was in doubt. As soon as Emma and Berkman were released in September 1919, federal authorities began the deportation process. When it became clear that Berkman would be deported, Emma chose not to pursue her legal options to remain in America.

Upon her discharge from prison, Emma stopped in Chicago to see Ben and his new family. In her autobiography she wrote that during her twenty-one-month imprisonment, she had come to peace with her feelings towards Ben. While that may have been her conscious perception, a sense of injustice, later to be so bitterly released in writing *Living My Life*, also must have been present.

Whatever change in feelings the future held, Emma was extremely generous at the time of her deportation. Despite Ben's speech renouncing anarchism for Christianity at her farewell dinner in Chicago—a message the Chicago anarchists never forgot nor forgave—Emma wrote him an appreciative letter from Ellis Island in December 1919:

> I was glad to have been in Chicago and to see you again, dearest hobo. I never realized quite so well how far apart we have traveled. But it is alright, nothing you have done since you left me, or will yet do, can take away the 10 wonderful years with you. . . . I have loved you much. But I have been rewarded not only in pain but in real joy—in ecstasy—in all that makes life full & rich & sparkling. I really owe much to you. During our years together I have done my best and

most valuable work. . . . If I owe much heartache, much soul-tearing misery to you, what of it? Nothing in life can be achieved without pain. I am glad to have paid the price. I only hope I too have given you something worth whatever price you have paid for your love. I shall feel proud and glad.

Arriving in Russia, Emma and Berkman quickly became disillusioned with the Communist government. They left two years later for a precarious life of exile and activism in Europe. Eventually, they settled apart in Southern France, Berkman with a fellow refugee, Emmy Eckstein, and Emma alone. Emma later married a Welsh anarchist admirer to obtain British citizenship. As a result, she had more freedom to travel and continue speaking and organizing than Berkman, who was constantly threatened with deportation from France.

My father wrote of Emma in the "Outcast Narratives":

For a quarter of a century she went through the country
Pleading, preaching, agitating
That the people get rid of Gods, capitalism and govern-
    ments.
America deported Emma Goldman to Soviet Russia
Where there was no government, God or capitalism.
After two years she said, "Nothing can be more terrible
Than to realize your early dreams."

EIGHT

Her Fragrant Ashes
Rest in My Bedroom Now

> If you will remember, Evans, you gave me a photograph
> some 20 years ago, and you wrote on it, "Anna
> Martindale made a man of you." It was much more true
> than you thought.
>
> —Ben Reitman to William Evans, 1939

While my father's public and professional life during his
years with Anna Martindale is well documented, there is only
a tantalizing glimpse of their private lives. During their early
years together, Ben's mother, Ida, took care of the baby and
the household, and Anna helped support the family through
her business as a dressmaker.

Anna was good at managing her own finances and
encouraged Ben to be more businesslike. Ben wrote her in the
late 1920s, "I'm ambitious to push up our savings account
now. I think I can prove that I can bank more money than
you." Anna gave up her dressmaking business as Ben's income
increased, but her foresight in purchasing a $5,000 life insur-
ance policy for herself suggests that she recognized her
economic importance to the family.

Anna and Ben were rarely home at the same time, but she
shared an interest in his work and reform efforts. In addition
to spending long hours in his medical practice, Ben often
spoke in the evenings at Chicago's two large outdoor forums,

Bughouse Square and the Bug Club, at the Hobo College, and at radical clubs around the city. Anna accompanied him to meetings and dinners, bringing Brutus with her as he got older. She also had her own interests and maintained a strong connection with her anarchist friends on the East Coast. She and little Brutus vacationed every summer at Mill Hollow, an anarchist colony in East Almstead, New Hampshire.

Anna, Ben and Ida adored Brutus. In "Following the Monkey," Ben described his pleasure at providing Brutus with nutritious food, toys, and summer camp—advantages he had not known as a child. Given Anna's experience as a child laborer, this was likely to be true for her as well.

A fifth member was added to the family in 1922 when Ben's daughter Helen, whom he had not seen in fifteen years, appeared unannounced at one of his lectures at the Hobo College. Helen had just completed two years at the University of Missouri, and was riding the rails across the country. Her bobbed hair and soldier's uniform drew the attention of the police, who arrested her for male impersonation. As resourceful as her father, she sold the story of her reunion with Ben to one of the Chicago newspapers after some Chicago relatives bailed her out of jail.

Helen was quite taken with Ben on first impression. Despite his need for a haircut and shave, she found him "vivid, alive, awake . . . maintaining the utmost poise and remaining absolutely the master of the situation." She added, "Personally, I did not find him as obnoxious as I feared to find him." Shortly afterwards, Helen moved to Chicago to live with Ben and Anna and completed her journalism degree at Northwestern University.

After graduating, Helen moved to New York to pursue her career as a writer and changed her name to Jan Gay, her maternal grandmother's family name. She eventually published several children's books and a book on nudism,

On Going Naked. Ben visited her in New York, and she occasionally came to see Anna and Brutus during their vacations
in New Hampshire.

Ben's description of Anna in "Following the Monkey," as the
devoted wife and mother who was loved and appreciated by
her husband, sharply contrasts his friend Frank Beck's portrait
of their relationship in his book, *Hobohemia.* Ben's blatant and
unrelenting pursuit of other women, Beck concluded, "must
have eaten into her soul like wormwood." Of course, as a
Christian minister, Beck had his own perspective. Even he
admitted that Anna gave no outward indication this was true.
Beck described Anna as "a decent and proud mother, curiously unsensuous," and someone who "cared more for Doc
than he was able to care for her."

Unlike Ben's previous relationship with Emma, only a few
letters have been found from the thirteen years that Anna and
Ben lived together. Although it is risky to conclude that the
absence of correspondence fifty years later means no letters
were written, the content of Ben's letters suggests that Anna
did not write often during her vacations in New Hampshire.

More importantly, Ben and Anna had trouble communi-
cating when they were together. As bombastic and lively as
Ben was in public, he was often moody at home with his
"periodic gloom and depressions" over his "inability to live
big" and the confines of regular employment. Despite her
devotion to Ben and their son, Anna had difficulty expressing
her feelings or making a connection with him at some deeper
level. According to Ben, "Anna lived an inner life that I did not
share." In 1919 she wrote to Ben:

> You will admit they [your "Letters to a Wife"] are very imper-
> sonal. There isn't even a hand grasp in them, and then you
> see I don't fit the part of a wife very well—Why not try
> "Letters to a Lover—or is it too late—let us work out our

lives together as lovers. I want a comrade who believes in me and who is glad and proud.

While my father often told Anna that he loved and needed her, he was far more open with her than with Emma about his infidelity. During her first vacation alone with the baby, Ben wrote Anna that he was faithful to her in her absence "after a fashion." He complained:

Dear Little Wife:
I have been in hard luck lately.
You know me
I used to be lucky with women.
And any night I could go to some woman
Who would be kind to me.
You know what my smile and my poetry
Used to do to them. . . .
Lately, I ain't done so well.
The girls refuse me and the women turn me down.
And even my old women friends
Pass me up.
And the worst of it is
I don't get no encouragement to try.

Despite his infidelity, Ben's work remained a strong bond between them. He wrote to Anna, "I believe God has great work for me to do/ And I shall do it./ Would you rather have a good husband than to live with a messenger of God?"

Anna had bouts of illness, probably depression. After eight years together, Ben perceived that Anna's unhappiness and recurrent illness were related to their unsatisfactory relationship. He wrote to her on one of her vacations in New Hampshire:

If I were to describe myself I would say that I am "provocative" in that I am able to make friend and enemy talk. Not so with you. Instead of drawing you out, I freeze you. Anna Lover, do you know what my feelings are when I have a "bad case" and the girl hovers between life and death? I die with her and suffer all her pains and more. So it is that I have a consciousness that I freeze and crush your soul.

When questioned about her unhappiness, Anna may or may not have mentioned Ben's infidelity—given her convictions about free love—but she did write that she resented Ida's interference in their lives. At first Ben was unwilling to show a preference for Anna over his mother. However, Anna and Brutus's absence and her rare letters made Ben think it over. Finally, he was able to make a choice. "I see the little Mother working around the house *happy* in her desire to serve me," he wrote. "I think of your great unhappiness because of her & I wonder about it all. I think when you return Mother will live at Olson's and we will have a full time servant girl." This willingness to choose Anna over his mother, when he had not done so for Emma, gives substance to my father's agreement with his friend William Evans that Anna Martindale had made a man of him.

In many ways the 1920s with Anna were my father's peak years professionally and physically. The largest source of patients for his growing medical practice were prostitutes— workers in a bustling Chicago business. My father was not the only one in Chicago to prosper from prostitution. Mob-run houses of prostitution supported civic authorities through payoffs at every level as well as hotel and rooming-house owners, pimps, tavern and cabaret owners, and taxi drivers.

Prostitutes also kept the Chicago Health Department busy. Starting in the early 1920s, the department began to quarantine, isolate, and hospitalize persons, primarily women, who had venereal disease. Women who tested positive for venereal disease in the Woman's Court Clinic were sent to Lawndale Hospital for periods of two weeks to two months. If an infected woman worked in a house of prostitution, the Health Department would placard the building with a large red sign, "Venereal Disease—Keep Out," sure to be bad for business.

Ben estimated that between 1920 and 1930, he saw more than 50,000 prostitutes, usually for the examination or treatment of venereal disease. He was more or less respectably employed doing examinations in the city and county jails, and in the Woman's Court Clinic. Through his ties to Chicago's underworld, for a time he was also the "line doctor," or house physician, for several houses of prostitution run by one of Al Capone's mobsters, Jack Zuta.

Ben examined several hundred women a week in these houses, and many of them became his private patients. Ben was always ready to mix business with pleasure. His semi-weekly visits to the houses were the occasion for "much zestful conversation, indiscriminate caresses and professional excesses." If Ben himself ever became infected with venereal disease from his activities, he did not mention it in his letters.

With the vice crackdowns in Chicago in 1923 and 1924, many syndicate houses went out of business. However, prostitution remained widespread in Chicago until, Ben would later write, it was hard even for prostitutes, their pimps, and tavern owners to do business in the Depression.

In 1924 Ben was offered a hotel that had been used as a "first class sporting house" by its discouraged mobster owners. Formerly employing forty women and visited by over a thousand men a day, according to Ben, the Granville had been subject to intense police raids, arrests, and fines. Idealistically, my father took up the offer with the idea of making it a hobo residence and a "humanizing experiment." For the time that it was in his care, the sign on the door read: "God's Kingdom for Hobos—Free Lodging and Meals for Hobos." The mobsters supplied food and clothing for the residents, and "all day and all night there were discussions about labor and ideals."

Ben's vision of a "church and university" for hoboes was short-lived. The neighbors, who had tolerated the previous guests without qualms, objected to the hobo tenants. Following legal action and extensive coverage in the newspapers, "God's Kingdom for Hobos" went out of business a month after it opened.

Ben's notoriety and the ensuing complaints about his activities at the Granville came to the attention of Dr. Herman Bundesen, the man who had replaced John Dill Robertson as commissioner of the Chicago Board of Health in 1922. Bundesen warned Ben to stay away from the vice lords and hoboes and, to prove he was serious, gave him a sixty-day leave of absence without pay. The two men remained on friendly terms, however, and shared a strong interest in venereal disease. Shortly after Bundesen was appointed commissioner, Ben took him and Dr. Evans on a tour of several houses of prostitution to discuss preventive measures.

By the mid-1920s my father felt strongly that the key to controlling venereal disease was prevention.

> The sex urge cannot be controlled, whether the individual is an anti-social vicious pimp or a cultured, thoughtful gentleman. There is only one hope, and that is prophylaxis. . . . There seems to be a feeling that those who indulge must take their chances, as if the danger would keep them from indulging! Such foolish notions only sanction the spread of venereal disease.

Ben preferred economic self-interest to regulation. He argued that neither treatment, whether compulsory or voluntary, nor the morals courts or other legal avenues set up to combat vice would ever halt the spread of venereal disease. In *The Second Oldest Profession* Ben noted that pimps recognized disease prevention would keep their women employed. Pimps were willing to show their "girls" how to prevent infection by douching and using prophylactic ointments. The women, in turn, could teach their "johns" to wash their genitals, void after contact, and use prophylactic ointments. As evidence that prevention was good for business, Ben pointed out that some houses even advertised their guarantee: "We pay for the treatment of any man infected with venereal disease in this house."

My father and Commissioner Bundesen had key political differences. Bundesen strongly supported prophylaxis in his early years, but he was also politically astute and destined for a long and productive career in public health in Chicago. In the face of public pressures against supporting "immoral behavior," Bundesen diverted the Health Department from emphasizing prevention of venereal disease and, instead, promoted placing signs in the houses of prostitution and hospitalization of infected women. Ben and Bundesen would have a complex personal and professional relationship for almost twenty years. Their differences would resurface dramatically in the Syphilis Control Program in the late 1930s.

In addition to his many other activities, my father also had literary aspirations. Always conscious of their role in history, both my father and Emma Goldman began thinking seriously in the mid-1920s about writing their autobiographies. After leaving Russia for France, Emma maintained an infrequent but affectionate correspondence with Ben. In 1926 Ben made arrangements to see her and show her his draft manuscript while he and Anna were in England visiting Anna's family. After having dinner with Emma, Ben wrote to Anna that Emma "is positively the most bitter and dejected person in the world. God save us from bitterness." Emma offered suggestions on his autobiography but, despite Ben's encouragement, was unwilling to reestablish sexual relations. Ben commented laconically, "She is gloomy, wants me about her (but not close)." Ben's autobiography went through several revisions, including one paid for by Ben's friend, William Evans, but was never published.

After Ben's visit to England, he and Emma continued to correspond on friendly terms. Ben saw her again in 1927 when she came to Canada to lecture and begin working seriously on her own autobiography, later to be titled *Living My Life*. At her request, Ben loaned her the passionate love letters she had written to him and his copies of *Mother Earth* magazine. After rereading her letters, Emma asked Ben to promise he would not use them in his book. Ben agreed: "The worst I would do would be to try and shine in a little of your reflected glory." Shortly afterward, Emma returned to France to continue working on her book. My father's dream of an autobiography would reappear in several forms over the years.

In 1928 my father's income from his medical practice was at its highest point. He made almost as much in one month as he would later make in a full year during the worst of the Depression.

He was also at his peak physically. Twelve-hour days in his office, followed by evening tours and lectures, were common. At fifty, there was no mention of the diabetes and nephritis that would later plague him. During the summer months Ben swam in Lake Michigan for an hour or more each day. Often a crowd followed him along the shore as he swam and he would give an impromptu speech when he got out of the water. He was also a member of the Chicago Polar Bear Club and would occasionally swim with friends in the icy winter lake.

The last glimpse of my father's life with Anna comes from an exchange of letters written in 1928, after eleven years of living together. My father's biographer, Suzanne Poirier, has interpreted Anna's final sense of peace with Ben as the result of her abdication of an emotional partnership, "becoming instead a caretaker of his physical and emotional health."

My own interpretation of Anna's change, admittedly based on my own experience with middle age, is that it was not caused by withdrawal, but by a maturation process. I prefer to think that, at forty-three, she accepted the reality that Ben would not change, and discovered she could control her own happiness. Despite Ben's unfaithfulness, Anna appears to appreciate their need for one another. Possibly the preference Ben showed her over Ida and her own intense maternal feelings for Brutus made Anna more tolerant of Ben's relationship with his mother.

In the summer of 1928, Ben acknowledged Anna's responsibility for his business and professional success as well as providing his "security, home, haven." He wrote:

> My weakness, my multiple emotions and needs almost kill me.
> The Gods do take care that trees don't grow into the sky.
> And they have seen to it that the joy and security you give me
> Cannot be duplicated by any other woman.
>
> And the love that is mine for you
> Make it impossible to have utter abandonment with anyone else.
> You haunt me, you hold me,
> Yet the "FORCES" draw me, draw me, temporarily take me.
> But always and always I come back to you.

Ben also wrote that he was ready to make out a will leaving everything to her and, for her protection, "there should be a legal law ceremony."

Anna was unusually open in her feelings about Ben in her letters that summer. She wrote, "I wonder if you feel as I do that 'we belong' and to no one else in the world." As to his suggestion about marriage:

> The thing that has held us together through the years has been your work in the outside world and the sense in which I have been able to stand by and help. We have a boy I care for . . . & work for & I helped get started in the world. If you would be happier if the seal of the law secured this contract of the spirit, it is all right—but I would hate publicity concerning it. . . .

However, there was no further correspondence about marriage and the matter was apparently dropped.

When Sarah Watchmaker, the mentally unstable woman whom Ben had befriended for years, attacked another woman who had been watching him swim, Ben finally had her committed to an institution. Anna cautioned him about his relationships with other women: "It was inevitable that something like this would happen as long as she was seeing you . . . I would say be careful, be careful how you stir the emotional life in others. Others cannot rebound the way you do."

The end of my father's and Anna's life together came suddenly. At forty-five, Anna became pregnant and had an abortion. Longing for "a quiet life," perhaps she thought she was too old or too ill to start again with a new baby or with such an undependable partner. The abortion might only have been part of a larger pattern of birth control. Anna and Ben had only one child in thirteen years of living together. Abortions, even though illegal, were a common method of birth control during that time for women who could afford them.

Following her abortion, Anna developed an infection which spread rapidly. Knowing she was dying, her last request concerned Brutus. She asked Ben to arrange for their son to go to her friends in New Hampshire in the event anything happened to him. Within a few days she was dead. After the autopsy, Ben was accused by the police of performing the abortion but was exonerated following an investigation.

Rev. Frank Beck officiated at Anna's funeral service describing it later as "so far different from the usual burial service that it might have been considered a travesty." Despite Ben's attempts at jocularity with his friends and his choice of a blues singer, "currently filling an engagement at a 'men only' sexy playhouse," Beck was touched by Ben's sadness. After the ceremony Ben followed the casket out into the street. Beck remembered, "With one arm Doc enfolds his treasured youthful son Brutus . . . the other arm is placed protectively and tenderly around the wasting body of his aging mother."

Anna's death changed my father's relationship to my half-sister Helen, by then known as Jan. Loyal to Anna and openly a lesbian, after Anna's death Jan became extremely critical of Ben and what she called the "whores" in his life. Despite her hostility, Ben wrote her frequently and the two continued to see each other on occasion. Fortunately, any bitterness Jan felt towards Ben did not extend to Brutus and she and her half-brother remained close.

After her death, Anna joined May and her baby as exceptions to my father's rule of "no regrets." "I used to weary you telling you how wonderful Anna was," he wrote to Emma two months after Anna died. "I never made her happy or was much of a husband. But oh I loved her and needed her so. Now only the memory of my denial lives on, with it ever increasing pain."

But as the pain of the early months receded, these regrets also became a way of generating sympathy from new women. Three years later he wrote to my mother about Anna:

I took her love, her devotion, the best years of her life.
And went on unthinking "having my fun where I found it"
Living my life and crushing her sweet life.

Her fragrant ashes rest in my bedroom now, and often in the
Stillness of the night when I hear my Son breathing in sweet
 sleep
And my stupidity and neglect to the one woman who
 LOVED ME comes
Back to me I reach out my arms to the UNKNOWN and
 "bow my head."

NINE

A Texan at Heart and an Alien Everywhere Else

Though she is an honest hard-working loyal mother and mate, fundamentally she is a native American, a conservative, a true Daughter of the South. But she is a genuine rebel when love came to her.

—*Ben Reitman to Theodore Schroeder, 1942*

If there was any surprise in reading hundreds of my mother's letters, it was that my overweight, white-haired, seemingly sexless mother had once been young. Of course, I knew this already in an intellectual way, having heard stories of her childhood and early career repeated many times as I was growing up. But to experience her life as a younger woman through her letters was another matter. To feel the fires that forged the strength in the older woman that I knew has been one of the great privileges of my life.

As my father often said in his letters, my mother, Medina Oliver, was indeed a Texan, despite living most of her life in Chicago. Her early life alternated between my great-grandmother's farm in Medina, Texas (hence her name) and life in the small Texas towns where my grandfather, Eugene Oliver, was a school administrator and my grandmother, Inez Baker Oliver, often taught school.

My mother entered the University of Texas as a fifteen-year-old freshman in 1919, majoring in science. Younger than most of her classmates, she did not date during college, but was active in sports and joined the football pep squad. My mother remained a loyal University of Texas alum all her life. When my sisters and I were small, she taught us all the Texas football songs and, during long car rides, we sang her college songs together.

Following a family tradition, she took a year off after her junior year to help support herself by teaching in a country school. At the end of the year, she and the local school board parted company by mutual agreement. Medina did not meet the school board's requirements for a "lady" schoolteacher. Although she changed into a dress at school, she was dismissed because she "wore riding britches to ride horseback to school and refused to ride side-saddle."

Medina entered the University of Texas Medical School in Galveston in 1924, one of four women in a class of eighty students. She did poorly her first year in anatomy and histology. Although she retook and passed the two courses successfully the following year, she felt out of phase with her classmates.

My mother lived in the women's dormitory, but had difficulty making close friends. She later described her feeling of isolation at that time to my father:

> I haven't the gift of being very happy. I am too much by myself. I do not make over one friend every twenty-five years. I suppose it is because people interest me and that is all, just interest. I can feel their pulse and put my ear to the ground and know what they think, but they do not like me for this ability.

A few male classmates tried to get to know her better, but my mother thought they were only looking for someone to support them through medical school.

Medina withdrew from medical school during the first

semester of her senior year. I can find only the briefest written reference to that painful senior year, a time she seldom talked about to my sisters and me. In one of her reminiscences, she wrote, "Dr. Keiller [a brilliant anatomist and dean of medical school] called me a fool and said that I had no fight." In a later letter of recommendation, Keiller's successor as dean described the situation more delicately: "Miss Oliver had considerable difficulty with Anatomy, in fact, so much so that she became discouraged and withdrew from the school." Her brother Gene remembers only that "she got into a wrangle with one of her professors and he told her he would see to it that she would never graduate. Papa went down to talk to him, but couldn't change anything."

My mother felt this loss of opportunity deeply. Four years after leaving medical school, she inquired about readmission. She was told that to be readmitted she would have to repeat several courses. She chose not to take this option. By 1939 she had negotiated with the school to take makeup exams only, and to take the preparatory courses in Chicago. But her dream of becoming a doctor was finally overcome by my father's death and her family responsibilities. She continued to be a lifelong student of anatomy. I remember her taking a fetal anatomy class after I graduated from college.

When my sisters and I were growing up, we assumed she had adjusted to the circumstances with equanimity. Thinking back now, her efforts in anatomy, as well as her silence about this period, suggest it was a loss she never fully accepted. On the rare occasion when we asked about her days in medical school, she would answer, "Many are called, but few are chosen." But all this was still far in the future when my mother left medical school and returned to Houston in 1928 to live with her family.

Her stay lasted a year. It could not have been easy living with my grandmother. Decades later my grandmother would instruct my sisters and me in money management by telling us tales of our mother's foolish spending. It was also not easy from my grandparents' perspective. My mother's feelings of anger and alienation are reflected in a later letter from her father: "I hope you avoid living your life apart this term as much as you did last," he wrote. "And I hope you come to feel like one of us more and more and be more interested in the family than you have seemed to be in the past."

My father once described my mother in a letter to my grandmother as "a Texan at heart and an alien everywhere else." He underestimated how much my mother felt an alien in Texas too. She had strong roots to her extended Texas family and her heritage, but she still felt a need to strike out on her own, to be somewhere and do something that she wasn't quite sure of. In recalling that youthful period she would quote a line she had heard from a Galveston minister, "Come when you can, sister, and leave when you must."

At twenty-five, my mother left Houston with the idea of selecting a graduate school (or possibly a medical school) at one of several Southern universities. Dissatisfied with what she saw, she impulsively drove north, arriving at the University of Chicago in the fall of 1929.

During her first winter in Chicago as a graduate student in bacteriology, my mother signed up for a sociological tour of the city. These "Reconciliation Trips," sponsored by the Methodist Church, were designed to introduce participants to Chicago's economic, social, and political problems during the Great Depression.

The tour she chose—to West Madison Street, Chicago's home in the 1930s for hoboes and honky tonks—was led by Rev. Frank Beck, my father's friend and fellow sociologist. My mother left her car in front of the Field Museum to go with Beck and the other participants on the streetcar. My father, a frequent speaker on Beck's tours, was speaking that day on "The Homeless Man."

Beck has described Ben during this period as "a superb

showman . . . his swaggering three hundred pounds, a long graceful cape over his shoulders when cold, always an over-sized walking stick in hand, his exotic picturesque figure commanded a passage through any crowded city street."

Despite my father's showy appearance, my mother did not pay much attention to him until she returned to her car and was trying to open the door. Her description of their first meeting and early relationship summarizes what became my favorite story from my childhood. She wrote about it later:

It was quite a chilly day and I had forgotten my gloves... A large, burly man in a sloppy overcoat who had been walking along with us and talking vociferously. . . . asked me where I was from, sister, took my hand and put it in his pocket. My story to our children is that he could never get the hand out. His wife [Anna] had just died and he was a diabetic and nephritic. He wondered if I was a nurse. I said I wasn't really but that I didn't mind study.

In writing down her love story, my mother aptly commented, "I have told it so many times it can be condensed." In the condensed version from my childhood, my father was intimately involved in her decision to enter nursing school in New York two years after she met him. She wanted to take care of him and "his diabetes and nephritis were giving him black and dangerous moods."

However, her first letters to my father from nursing school in March 1932 reveal that there was a great deal about him that my mother did not know. Many women had preceded her in loving Ben, including one he had married nine months earlier! Rev. Beck performed the ceremony, after first warning Rose Siegel, the prospective bride, against marrying a man with my father's history and character.

TEN

The Fates Give Us Our Wives

I married Rose because she waited 20 years for me and
my mother wanted me to do it. I never really loved Rose.
—*Ben Reitman to Theodore Schroeder, 1942*

Of all the "other" women in my father's life, Rose Reitman is
the only one that I remember meeting. When I was twenty-
one and in my first job as an elementary school teacher in
New York, she came to my school by chance as a substitute
teacher. When I heard the new teacher's name, I was both
curious and eager to find extended family in a strange city.
Naively, I introduced myself to her as Ben Reitman's daughter
and asked if we were related. She replied abruptly, "I'm no
relation to those Chicago Reitmans," and walked away.

I called my mother in Chicago about my experience and
she was equally succinct. "Stay away from Rose," she advised
me. "She'll only cause trouble!" Characteristic of my early reluctance to face the past, I never asked why or made any effort
to contact Rose again. By the time I was ready to learn more,
thirty years later, she was dead.

When I first began to read my family's letters, I wanted to
believe the worst of the woman who I thought had made my
mother's life so difficult. Getting to know Rose through her
letters surprised me. Middle class, a conscientious teacher,
and a woman eager to find fulfillment as a wife and mother,
she was someone I might have related well to in my own late
thirties. Fortunately, I have been spared Rose's twenty-year

optimism for the heights that marriage to someone like my father could offer, and the depths of her despair and rage so shortly after she succeeded.

Little is known about Rose's early life. Judging from allusions to her mother's sacrifices to send Rose and her brother to college, she was probably from a poor Jewish immigrant family. She and Ben met around 1915 in the *Mother Earth* office when she was a college student in New York. They became lovers and this relationship continued on an occasional basis in New York and Chicago during Ben's remaining years with Emma, for the thirteen years he lived with Anna Martindale, and for a year after Anna's death. However, until shortly before their marriage, there is nothing in Ben's remaining letters to suggest the significant role Rose would later assume.

The period following Anna's death was difficult for my father for a number of reasons. Adding to his loss were the public criticisms from his former radical comrades. The vindictiveness of their books made him uneasy about what Emma would say about him in the autobiography she was writing. Ben wrote to her:

Dearest Mommy.
Into these crowded days
Your presence comes often.
I have been wondering about you and your book.
You saw what Margaret Anderson wrote about me.
"The fantastic Dr. Reitman (who wasn't so bad if you
    could hastily drop all your ideas as to how human beings
    should look and act)" — You know I always liked
Margaret and thought she was friendly.
It was the same way about Harry Kemp. I liked and helped
    him, thought he was my friend, but in his book,
Tramping on Life, he called me "A big fat nincompoop."
Wonder what you will call me.

My father neglected to mention that Harry Kemp also described him as "such a weakling as great women must necessarily, it seems, fall for," a statement Emma's biographer, Candace Falk, finds typical of the jealousy and continued resentment of many of Emma's friends. When Ben was omitted in Hippolyte Havel's biographical sketch of Emma in *Anarchism and Other Essays*, their mutual friend, Agnes Inglis, wrote to Emma, "Did they all hate Ben or what? Ben is a sort of unmentionable person. But what a tremendous character. . . . Ben touches life way down. And while it isn't the way I want to touch it, it's the way he does and he does."

Agnes is one more example of how my father could strongly attract and then totally repel. It is a sad commentary that a woman like Agnes, who admired my father for years, eventually had enough of his behavior and broke off all communication with him.

Although Ben did not see Emma's manuscript until it was published, he had good reason to be worried about what she would say about him. Emma had undergone a significant change from the author of the affectionate letter she wrote in 1923, seven years after their physical relationship had ended. "Old Benie dear," she wrote, "you have been in my mind a great deal since I have had to leave America. Especially since I am out of Russia, I have thought of our work together and many many other things. I feel proud to have meant so much to you."

However, six more years of exile and the process of reviewing her life for her autobiography caused her to view Ben in a colder and more vengeful light. Emma's biographer, Alice Wexler, does an excellent job of examining Emma's complex motivation in the construction of her autobiography. According to Wexler, Emma's awareness "that I have nothing left in the way of personal relations from all who have been in my life and torn my heart" encouraged her to portray herself as the model of a courageous and self-sufficient woman. As she reread the hundreds of her love letters that Ben returned to her, her long-suppressed anger towards him finally came to the surface. At the same time, she deliberately omitted, or perhaps was unable to acknowledge, aspects of her own dependency which these letters revealed.

One of the more telling differences between Emma and my father was that, for all his dishonesty with women, my father wanted to let history judge the real man he had been. Emma, for all her contributions, chose to leave for posterity a persona different than who she really was. Before beginning her book she wrote to Alexander Berkman, "We all have something to hide. Nor is it cowardice which makes us shrink from turning ourselves inside out. It is more the dread that people do not understand, that what may mean something very vital to you, to them is a thing to be spat on."

Like many other Americans at the beginning of the Depression, by late 1930 my father's problems were increasingly financial. Both prostitutes and his legally employed patients were less likely to pay their bills. Equally important, without Anna, Ben was a poor manager of his money. When Dr. Florence Rego, an abortionist and former medical school classmate, needed to leave Chicago following the death of one of her patients, Ben readily advanced her part of his son Brutus's $5,000 inheritance. But, lucky as always, it was still a good investment for his future. This money became the down payment on Rego's small cottage in a modest neighborhood on Chicago's South Side.

Looking for another source of income, and inspired by Emma's literary efforts, Ben began work on a book about the subject he knew best: prostitutes and their pimps. When his interest in the project flagged, the completion of *The Second Oldest Profession* was substantially aided by the stability in his personal life provided by a new lover, twenty-two-year-old Retta Toble.

Although Retta lived with Ben, Brutus, and Ida for less than six months, it would be a critical relationship for my father. Described by Ben as "young, beautiful and playful," Retta was helpful both at home and in Ben's office, and was extremely deferential to the newly reinstated tyrant, Ida. Retta's parents were political radicals and sheep ranchers in South Dakota. Her mother had been a hobo years earlier and might have known Ben. Following her mother's example, Retta worked and traveled around the country for several years before arriving in Chicago.

My father's book was published the following spring. The dedication read: "I dedicate this book to Emma Goldman, the most brilliant and useful woman I have ever met. She taught me that men and women will never be free until they learn not to exploit or be exploited." Ben boasted to Emma before the book's release, "You are going to write a great autobiography. . . but my *Second Oldest Profession* will have a larger circulation and make more money than your new book. . . . Your immortality is assured because I dedicated my book to you."

Emma disagreed. She wrote to Agnes Inglis, "Ben not only lacks the ability to write but he cannot enter into his subject deeply enough to bring up what he finds. He sees only the surface."

The Second Oldest Profession did not admit Ben to the inner circle of sociologists at the University of Chicago, in whose classes he frequently lectured. However, it was favorably reviewed and considered complementary to their sociological studies of Chicago. Emma also had a comment on that score. "That Ben is accepted in universities merely shows the shallowness of the American 'learned' profession," she wrote her current lover. "These people have helped very considerably to increase his self importance and his truly diseased craving to shine as a 'sociologist' and writer."

In the spring of 1931, Retta left for a family emergency, plan-

ning to return to Ben in Chicago. Whether it was by coinci-
dence or in response to a letter from Ben, within a week of
Retta's departure for South Dakota, Rose telegraphed Ben to
meet her in Pittsburgh or Buffalo. Something must have encouraged Rose to press her advantage because a few weeks
later Ben wrote her the following:

Dear Cautious Jew Rose.

You have survival qualities.
That is why you held your job for 14 years.
Why you didn't marry some worthless man.
Why you have saved a "pretty dollar"
Why you live on Riverside Drive. . . .

And you have gotten along so well without me.
Never were you a more beautiful woman.
Never were you so well off.
Never were your chances of marrying well, better.
Never was your future so bright.
A happy trip to Honolulu, every thing your heart needs.

Now as to me.
I do want to be honest. . . . I think I know how to be.

> "I can only say the things I feel
> I can only sing my little song.
> For to admire and for to see the world so wide
> It never did much good to me.
> But I couldn't stop if I tried."

Still not discouraged, Rose came to Chicago at the beginning of her summer vacation. She was welcomed by Ida, who
saw a Jewish daughter-in-law as a preferable alternative to a
series of transient women like Retta, who would be a bad

influence on Brutus. Rose's subsequent letters express a genuine fondness for Brutus, warm relations with his mother, and a willingness to honor Anna's memory, all of which made her a good candidate for marriage, should Ben be so inclined.

Rose and my father married in July 1931 when she was thirty-eight and he was fifty-two. It was a stormy marriage from the beginning. Rose's sympathy towards Ben in her role as "the other woman" vanished when her position was reversed. Years later one of my cousins asked Rose why she had married Ben when she knew he had been unfaithful to Anna with her and she could reasonably expect the same. Rose replied, "I thought I could reform him."

Despite his marriage, Retta and Ben continued to correspond for several years, with Retta frequently extolling Ben's virtues as a friend and lover. Ben delighted in sharing Retta's letters with an infuriated Rose, who had nothing good to say about "that red rat Retta." Until the end of his life, my father would remember Retta fondly as the woman who gave him a book. Actually, it would be more correct to say she gave him two books. Retta's sense of adventure and her joyful acceptance of life's opportunities and disappointments made her one of the models for his heroine, Box Car Bertha, in *Sister of the Road*, my father's 1937 novel about a woman hobo.

My father's decision to drop an appealing young woman like Retta to marry Rose is typical of his impulsive reversals, yet it remains a mystery to me. He had offered prophetic comfort to his friend Nels Anderson a year earlier. "I suppose God knows his business," he wrote. "And while we select our friends, the fates give us our wives." Possibly Ben thought the accommodating Retta was too similar to Anna. Perhaps pressures from Ida to find a mother for Brutus, along with Rose's long-term loyalty and willingness to serve, caught him at a weak moment, as he claimed. Despite his denial later, there was certainly a bond between my father and Rose. After he had not seen Rose for a year, he wrote a former lover, "She

[Rose] has a strange hold on me. . . . I suppose she always will. I never knew I was such a coward about women."

Ben's inability to make a living, in addition to his open infidelity, compounded the problems of his new marriage. Despite the time he spent with his patients, his income continued to decline. No longer on either the public health or mobster payrolls, his office was filled with what Roger Bruns describes as "an incredible assortment of homeless men and women, unemployed mothers, dope addicts, whores, pimps, pickpockets and bootleggers, all displaying an array of personal problems sufficient to fill sociological volumes."

Ben and Rose also had to deal with the publication of Emma's autobiography in the fall of 1931. When *Living My Life* was released, Ben was shocked by Emma's characterization of him as a thief, a coward, and the villain in their relationship. He wrote to her in December:

My Dear Mommy.

For a month I have been ill.
And in the depth of despair.
As you so often put it.
"You were sitting on my chest choking me."
Never in my whole life was I so outraged, humiliated, bitter, disappointed and crushed,
And never was I so near coming back at you.
In a way I should have regretted all my life.
You wrote your book, it is finished, you "were honest"
And "true to yourself," so that is all that is needed.
I am doing a good many talks on your book and I shall review it soon.
And you will see I HAVE BEEN LOYAL AND FAITHFUL TO YOU. . . .
Living My Life cost me 20 pounds, I lost my big belly, thanks.

Emma was not above boasting to Agnes Inglis, "He tells me I have taken all the bombast and egoism out of him. I wish it were true, then I should consider it a great accomplishment, but I am afraid that Ben will die as he lived, believing himself abused by those who cared for him most. It can't be helped. Perhaps none of us gets out of our skin."

Emma's own failure to "get out of her skin" in her autobiography is well-documented by her biographers, Candace Falk and Alice Wexler. She denied any intention to hurt Ben and argued that some reviewers misinterpreted her book. "By no manner of means could any sane person interpret his [Ben's] taking money as thievery," she wrote one editor.

Although Rose had her furniture moved from New York to Chicago after her marriage to Ben, she was prudent enough not to sever her relations with the New York City school system. Concerned when her $1,000 savings were half gone, she returned to New York before the end of the year. According to my mother, Rose never intended to stay in Chicago longer than a school semester. "When Rose's sabbatical was over, she took her Oriental rug and went home," she told us. What my mother omitted was that, for the next three years, Rose and Ben continued to live together on his frequent visits to New York and on her occasional visits to Chicago.

Rose expected that they would both commute until Ben could move to New York or his medical practice improved in Chicago. For years her letters expressing longing for him, self-pity for her sacrifices, and hope for the future typically alternated with letters of criticism and rage. She wrote the following message shortly after her return to New York:

> I want my Ben. I could cry out against God. Hasn't 15 years of torture been enough for me? Why am I being punished more than every creature? Give me my Ben. That's all I've cried for all my life. Does it all seem silly to you—whose sole

interest is either a sparkling mentality or just physical. What strange force is it. Will you ever mean anything but pain & anguish to me? I want peace and happiness with you so much. . . .

Tear up my letter. Nobody but *You* must know my secret and how much I love you.

In February 1932, a few months after Rose returned to New York, my mother entered the St. John's School of Nursing on Long Island, New York. In a letter written a month after her arrival, she addressed Ben formally as Dr. Reitman and took the news of his recent marriage to Rose in the spirit of a younger, admiring acquaintance. My mother's concern about his health, her lack of sympathy for his politics, and her encouragement to him to save his marriage would be consistent themes in her letters.

She wrote in that first letter:

Why don't you give your wife a chance? I had not heard of your last marriage. I know that you have known and studied thousands of women, and you understand them after a fashion. But if your wife loves you, she would change her God, her heaven, and her people to suit your taste. I feel like a calf tied outside the corral of yours and her difficulty.

Although Ben showed Rose many of his letters from women, Rose did not perceive Medina as a threat at this time. Her concern was with the "red headed girl," Retta. Ben saved only the last two pages of one of Rose's eighteen-page letters, but the preceding pages were probably similar. Like her predecessors, Rose understood where she stood relative to Ida. She wrote:

The truth is you have only your *Mother*—the mother that

you curse for bringing a Jewish girl into your house. She is your only fortress. It is she who holds your inward being together. Oh yes. I know you see yourself as the hero of some great movement when she is away & Brutus on his own—and a red-headed girl to pipe sweet words of glory to you. . . . If you have given up your Retta . . . then tell me so.

Ben, Brutus, and Rose were together for a summer camping trip and Rose returned to New York for the start of the new school term in a hopeful mood. Ben had applied for a license to practice medicine in New York and Rose reminded him about his responsibilities:

Yes Ben, you care for the desolate. . . . Your heart is drained by the pathos you encourage about you. Strong tho you may be—these leeches sap dreadfully. Consequently you turn to all sorts of hokus pokus to refuel. You are bright and good but . . . your proportion of 9/10 love of the world and 1/10 love of your family is an inverted ratio reacting grievously on yourself. . . . Try and make an opportune path out of this love for the downtrodden, but no one pair of shoulders or one brain can bear what your office sees in a day.

Once she began to price medical office space in New York, Rose was even more explicit. "I want you to deal with people that at least can justly compensate for your skill," she wrote. "I want material security—for the sake of health & helpfulness to others and cheer. Were it not material need I shouldn't be away from you. I fear it."

That fall, Ben received a letter from the New York Board of Medical Examiners rejecting his application for a license because of his expulsion from medical school thirty years earlier. With prospects for Ben's employment in New York stymied, and with Rose getting word from her Chicago friends that he had married her for her money and was reading her letters to other women, she asked for a divorce.

My father replied, more or less truthfully:

> Your specific charge that I married you for your money was made against me and proven thirty years ago by May Reitman. I can furnish you with the divorce proceedings and clippings from the Golden Ill. and San Diego papers to prove it. . . .

> I have been expelled from College, disbarred from Medical Societies, thrown out of the Press Club, dropped from membership of a Church, kicked out of the Hobo College, thrown out of political meetings, refused membership to all of the best clubs and ordered out of many hotels. I have a reputation for being the most "vulgar man in America," a publicity hound, a dangerous revolutionist, a psychopathic personality, a charlatan, a fake clap doctor and many other things.

> I suggest that you make grounds for divorce: adultery, brutality, non support, desertion, incompatibility and cruelty.

> I will not oppose your desire for freedom, pay all expenses and agree to any kind of settlement or alimony.

The last line is probably an inadvertent error on my father's part, but was actually correct. His unwillingness to pay would always be the apparent point of failure in their years of arguments about a divorce.

However, it did not take Ben long to change his mind. Playing on Rose's love for Brutus, he wrote a few days later, "I am absolutely honest. I want my son to be honest. And I want him to know his Father is honest." He added, "I did not take your request for a legal separation seriously./ I felt it was a mood and that you did not mean it./ And expect you most any time to write me a beautiful letter/ Saying I was your husband love and all you wanted in your whole life."

He was right. Not only was Rose ready to forgive him, but she was also willing to forgive herself for her relationship with Ben while he was with Anna. She wrote:

> When I was unrighteous years ago even before I compre-hended what I did—I cut out my heart but I did not blot my conscience. Now I don't want you to wrong me or anyone else—for your sins are on my soul too—and I'd rather not live, than live with knowing wrongs and sins on my soul.

> I think you ought to be in New York. Leave off your non-sense with this one or that. It leaves only a bad aftermath. Take only what God meant for you.

> Tell me much of Brutus. Yesterday I saw a tall young boy—slender as he is—& tears started to my eyes. Brutus is a big boy—but he is still my dream baby.

> I'm expecting you so long I'm wondering how long.

Ben did come to New York to see the waiting Rose over the Christmas holidays in 1932. He also arranged to spend time with my mother and it was at this point that they became sexually intimate. At the end of my mother's life, when she was bedridden and in a great deal of pain from cancer, she would reminisce to me about happier days when she and my father had first "done bedroom work." In that first experience, she was left unsatisfied when my father was finished. "Have you ever read Havelock Ellis?" she asked him. Despite several wives and hundreds of lovers, Ben Reitman still had much to learn about a woman's sexual response.

ELEVEN

A Correspondence School
for Breaking Hearts

For almost a decade Eileen has given me a love and devotion that I have never known before. . . . I hope Eileen
will write the story of our love and our work together.
                    —*Ben Reitman to Theodore Schroeder, 1942*

When the letters from Eileen O'Connor's trunk came to light
in 1992, over fifty years after my father's death, the explanation for such a rich cache was also among them in one of the
newly discovered boxes. In a small spiral notebook that Eileen
had used as a diary, she noted she was storing women's letters
to Ben, along with her own first letters from Ben, to use in
writing his biography after his death. Her trunk was kept in
the basement of Ben's house in Chicago. Somehow, when my
brother and his wife boxed and stored the enormous collection of my father's papers after his death, two cartons with
the contents of her trunk became separated from the rest.
Although Eileen searched for her letters among Ben's papers
after his death, she could not find these boxes.

Of all my father's voluminous correspondence, his early
letters to Eileen have the greatest power to make me angry,
even after many readings. Far more trusting and naive than
my mother (who was aided by an early warning from a friend
that Ben was "simply devoid of principle," and who did not
take him seriously), Eileen seems so hungry for love. And yet,
as I reread the letters, my outrage at my father's exploitive

behavior is tempered by this opportunity to know Eileen. I am fascinated by her willing decision to go to him and, eventually, to stay.

Written over a short period of time, these letters to Eileen show my father at his most enticing worst. His rich talent for motivating others (or manipulating them, depending on your point of view) lay in his uncanny ability to pick up on cues that told him exactly what the other person wanted to hear. The letters are also a unique opportunity to know my father. Unlike his business correspondence, Ben generally did not save carbons of his typed letters to women, and many were handwritten. My mother would not return his letters when he asked for them.

Comparing these letters to my father's correspondence with Emma twenty years earlier, I find it easier to identify with the lonely and inhibited Eileen. I can imagine her fears and inhibitions, deliciously broken down inch by inch, far more readily than I can the emotions of the passionate and (usually) self-assured Emma.

Ben's letters to Eileen are not sexually explicit like his letters to Emma, but they are just as evocative. For me, Gold-man biographer Alix Shulman's comment about Emma and Ben's correspondence applies here: "To read the sometimes sappy, often moving, ever scandalous love letters . . . is to ride the roller coaster of True Romance."

Eileen had hoped to tell her own love story but did not have the opportunity. While it is not the love story I would want, it is certainly a true love story with a happy ending for Eileen, as well as for Ben. If Eileen's spirit is still hovering over the boxes of her letters, I hope it will find my version of her story satisfactory.

Eileen was raised in a large Irish Catholic family in Ontario, Canada, near the Buffalo, New York border. Her domineering (and probably alcoholic) father was "feared and hated" by her mother. Eileen had gone to work at the age of sixteen to help support her family. She described herself as shy: "From my earliest childhood I have feared trespassing— being where I was not wanted and did not belong." Those who knew her in Chicago confirm that she was "plain, quiet and unassuming." But, like Anna, her boldness in taking Ben on as a partner and her tenacity in hanging onto such a painful and stormy relationship make these descriptions deceptive.

In 1933, when Eileen was forty-five, she had been working in Buffalo as a medical secretary for a number of years. Never married, she dreaded becoming a "barren old woman," and was looking for ways to give her life more meaning. At one point she had considered working in a leper colony. After reading about Ben in a magazine, she wrote to him asking about "Living with Social Outcasts," his forthcoming book mentioned in the article. Ben was always ready to answer a new woman's letters, particularly one so sympathetic to the new book he was just starting. After the first few letters, the two wrote each other almost daily. Ben also kept other women posted on his efforts to involve Eileen in his new project. "Surely you have not started a correspondence school for breaking hearts," one commented.

So few of Eileen's letters from this period were in the boxes, I assume she found them in her search and took them back. But their loss is not critical. Both Eileen and Ben come alive in my father's letters. He wrote on Washington's birthday, 1933:

My Dear Lady.

. . . I am hard at work on my "Living with Social Outcasts"
There will be five volumes and it will be
   Autobiographical . . . .
If you were in Chicago I would take you for a walk along
   the lake
And tell you about it. (That is if you would go)

No, Young Lady, working for "human welfare" a better world
Is not "heartbreaking." It is beautiful, the most worth while
Activity in life.
And the world is getting better.
The old system Capitalism is gone
And the glorious thing about it is that you and I can have
A real part in building a Society without Social Outcasts.
Poverty and unemployment.

By March 8th Ben was already tentatively asking "My dear
Irish Lassie" for her assistance with his book. He wrote:

Your letter "wakes the fever in my bones" I want to write
A powerful inspired book "Living with Social Outcasts and
Those who deal with them." I have the great opportunity of a
Life time, I have the material, the illumination, the desire.
Now I need strength, love, someone to help, to soothe to
   stand by.
I wonder if to do GREAT INSPIRED WORK we must be
   lonely, miserable.

By March 16th Ben was writing to "Dearest Eileen." After
first warning her that "Ben . . . can never be the true/ lover of
one woman, he can never be faithful to anything," he continued:

Oh Eileen I haven't told you the half.
I just tell you one thing.
You make me happy, wild delirious I want to sing I
Want to fly to you and pluck a few stars and lay them in your
Lap. You Irish Darling I love you for what you already
Have done for me. Get me. Already done to me. My book
Will be different better because you said a few kind words to
   me.

All my fears and doubts are swept away. . . .

Darling Eileen . . . the Gods knock at our door.
Service, beauty, greatness, fame await us.
All your loneliness, all my misery, all our prayers
Were not in vain, the hour has struck and we cry together.
Here we are Lord, send us.

On March 18th, encouraged by what he called her "newsy, breezy, gossipy letters," Ben clarified that he was also looking for physical love, but with a "spiritual mate, someone who can climb the mountains and step from star to star with me."

On March 25th, shortly over a month after they had begun corresponding, Ben wrote Eileen that he had heard from his publisher that he would be receiving a contract to produce a complete manuscript of "Living with Social Outcasts" within 90 days. Asking Eileen to come to Chicago to help him, Ben then offered her his own version of a contract. He also suggested that she meet him first for a day before she made up her mind. He wrote:

Do you Eileen O'Connor after serious meditation and
    believing your self sane and rational solemnly agree
To leave your home, family, a good job, respectability, an
    honorable
Past and with your eyes open enter into association with
A notorious Anarchist, FreeLover, Agitator and Champion of
    Social Outcasts.
Do you willing and deliberately enter into an alliance with a
Man who has a prison record, a shady past, a list of unhappy
    women
A wife he has deserted.

Do you after knowing that the Man is old, has false teeth,
Is afflicted with several ailments, has all kinds of bad habits

Is unable to make a living, has debts.

Do you after knowing all these things want to come to
    Chicago
And work on a book to be called "Living with Social
    Outcasts".
And take a part of any money that the Author may honestly
    earn.

Do you after understanding that this offer is a temporary one
And that after the book is finished about July 1st.
The Author may decide to do most anything and will have
    no
Obligations to you other than those you can provoke in him.

If you can fully, freely and happily accept all these conditions
If you can forsake all and follow me knowing that the road
Before you is most difficult and uncertain.
Then come to me.

He wrote in the accompanying letter, "Such a decision
came to me one day./ and I left all and followed Emma
Goldman./ I have always had occasion to be glad I did it." He
added, "Let us not be melodramatic, you have been looking
for a/ big kick in life. Now you have it."

Eileen's hesitation, particularly about the state of Ben's
finances, caused him to answer on March 27th:

Thank you for thinking I can make OUR living.
I have always been able to make a good living.
When I was with Emma Goldman we earned from $25,000
    to $75,000 a year.
Her speeches and my organization and hard work did it.
She always got all of the money, that went into her propa-
    ganda.

But we will fear no evil. I really have less than $1,000.00 in
   debts.

Eileen later recalled this final period of indecision. In
praying for guidance, she opened the Bible that Ben had given
her. "I slipped my hand into the Bible and asked for a 'guide',"
she remembered, "and the verse came 'I find no fault with this
man.'" Eileen agreed to meet Ben for a weekend in Detroit.
   In one of her few surviving letters from this period, Eileen
wrote that she would not take a leave of absence from her job,
but instead, planned to resign. She added:

And don't worry, my Ben. If you can't accept me, I'll always
be all right. But I think I know—I belong with you (not
conceit—I can't explain—just as you say, growing to each
other). . . .

Oh my dear, am I a simple fool! Say what you want to say to
me about yourself. I have your letters. And we are just new
and young together.

In his last letter before they met, Ben assured Eileen that
"he had never prayed so earnestly or longed so insistently/ to
be worthy of the love and confidence you have bestowed
upon me." Holding out the additional hope that she might
have a child, he concluded his letter:

Darling all our letters have been so spontaneous, it has been
So easy to write and to love you.
You pushed everybody out of my life.
The only one who might have claims, Rose, is fading into the
   dim
Past. You alone have the center and the whole stage. . . .

You shall have a most comfortable home in Chicago.

And then this summer when things are adjusted
And we are sure we belong then maybe we can make
    arrangements
For Brutus's little Sister.

Of everything my father wrote to Eileen in these early months, his statement that the letters were spontaneous and easy to write rings the most true. My father did not have to think about what he was writing. Lines like "Eileen, Eileen, look the doves are flying straight toward/ the golden sun," rolled off his tongue and out of his typewriter.

Ben was in love, not with the woman Eileen, but with the process of seduction. Unconcerned about the future, he was a man who lived in the moment. It would still be years before my father would learn the lesson of mutual dependency. Thinking of Eileen, he wrote years later, "Someone once said, 'Find them, F them, Feed them and Leave them.' But that don't work. People I work and play with have a habit of moving into my life. And they don't move out so easy."

Ben and Eileen met in Detroit and spent two days and a night together. It was probably her first sexual experience. Eileen recalled later to Ben, "You know when we faced each other in that room in the Tuller Hotel. You took off my hat and looked and looked at me. Then you kneeled with your arms all around me and held your face against my breasts. You couldn't know I was saying, 'Oh God, let me never fail him.'"

Unfortunately, my father's side of the story is told by his spiteful gesture towards his wife. Before leaving Detroit, he deliberately introduced Eileen to Rose's cousin, a local newspaper reporter, who (he was sure) would get the news back to her.

TWELVE

Choosing the Good Sower

Medina and I had a lovely romance. We were together
occasionally for three years. Most of the time she was
nursing in a hospital [in New York]. In the wonderful
nights together, Medina would say, "Make me a baby."
—*Ben Reitman to Theodore Schroeder, 1942*

In my mother's first letter after my father's visit during the
1932 Christmas holidays, a new theme appeared. She wrote:

Dear Dr. Reitman:
. . . It was good to look at you again. I like to see you; to feel
you close; to hear you, to smell and taste you. Sometimes my
breasts just sigh and my thighs ache but not for any other
man.

If I can arrange to get expelled for about a week at Easter I
shall come to Chicago. You know if the worst comes to the
worst I can always start a novena to the Holy Ghost, but
according to record that procedure has only been successful
once and there are those who doubt even that as authentic.

My mother continued to address my father as Dr. Reitman
for a year after they had become lovers. Such formality seems
surprising by today's standards, but I think it reflected her
awareness of their twenty-five year age difference and her role
as a minor character in my father's life. It was also consistent

with my mother's Victorian upbringing. One of her stories about her Grandmother Baker, whom she greatly admired, was that she always called her husband "Mr. Baker" even after ten children!

My mother's determination to have a child by my father, illustrated by her humorous allusion that making love to him was an alternative preferable to prayer, remains the most mysterious aspect of her life for me. Given how rarely they were together and the length of time her vision would take, it amazes me that she could be so single-minded. Babies would be a recurrent theme in her letters to Ben for the next three years. And she wanted, not only one, but two. "It would be the nicest thing I can think of to have twins and raise one for the control," she wrote Ben.

The reasons for my mother's decision to have Ben father her child are probably too complex for a daughter to appreciate—or too simple for me to believe. Unlike Anna, she was not philosophically committed to free love, nor was she in her mid-forties and childless like Eileen. Perhaps her feelings of isolation made her think she would never marry. It's possible that a child who would be "mine" and not "ours" might satisfy a woman with a desire for motherhood and yet a strong sense of independence.

There's no question that my mother loved my father and thought he was her destiny for motherhood. Despite their many differences, the qualities she admired in him were ones she wanted for her children. His indifference to social convention both appealed to her rebellious side and made him likely to accommodate her. Perhaps I look for reasons because I am uncomfortable with my mother's early intuition that "life and love will be generous to me." In the end, nothing that had happened would make her change her mind.

Medina's resonance with Ben made him the one person to whom she could express herself freely. Her letters to Ben thoroughly describe her experiences as a student nurse in a crowded, understaffed, Catholic city hospital and her thoughts about her past and her future. When she began working in the emergency room, she wrote him, "This place has three ambulances on call and in this neighborhood you can just imagine what they bring in. Of all the gore, and burns, and drunks, I can only begin to describe."

Although she and her parents exchanged weekly letters, Medina could not be open with them. She wrote Ben almost a year after she started nursing school, "I have never told them about entering this place. My letters to them are rather full of the weather." She may have considered nursing school further evidence of failure from someone who had wanted to become a doctor, one more project she might start and abandon, or perhaps she merely took a perverse pleasure in being secretive. She could, however, describe her affection for her parents to Ben: "They are well-meaning simple people; they are what you call distant people, but they are God's salt."

Although Medina was intensely in love with Ben, she recognized from the beginning it was one-sided:

> You have a sort of natural feeling of brotherhood for people that makes you such a wonderful person. Would that I could acquire a state with you where independence is equal, dependence mutual, and obligations reciprocal. I do not just love you—there is something about you I adore and that is all I have to give you.

It is clear to me now that, in sharp contrast to the stories my mother told me as a child, at the time my father considered her only one of several lovers while he was in New York, and a willing and entertaining correspondent. Far more than a sweetheart, he wanted help in the "Social Revolution," he wrote her. "What/ is needed now is Great Souls and Clear brains to/ help build a new and better than Russian Communistic Society." Unlike Eileen, Medina found this invitation an easy one to refuse.

Despite these differences, Medina remained convinced that Ben was the right man to be the father of her child. By the time she had progressed to addressing him by his first name, a year later, she was even more certain. She wrote:

> I think it is a stage similar to long division or wearing socks which one must pass through and on to something else. Now I ought to be in the stage of multiplying. The happiest life seems to be the one lived in others' lives. For me that would mean watching a little girl or boy wade, run, dig or explore; listening to laughter, talk, whistling, stamping; or hearing the loveliest word over and over, "mother." Any woman who realizes how wonderful children are and has any intelligence at all should want them. They give a sense of dignity and self value. To have a little silky-headed baby in a crib is a colossal joy. Ben darling, you can study any kind of woman existing: the nuns who have their religion, women with dramatic, literary or artistic success; you can see what divorce, remarriage, travel, solitary living or anything else does for them; but those who have sought happiness have daughters and sons.

It is poignant, yet amusing, for me to read my mother's letter now, because it was, indeed, a stage that she passed through before moving on to something else. When my sisters and I were teenagers in the 1950s, our family joke about Mother was that she was always taking classes or going somewhere, and was never home to take care of us.

Given what I now know about my mother's history, my sex education as a young woman also takes on new meaning. I do not think my mother could separate sex from reproduction either for her daughters or herself.

My youngest sister, Olive, once complained to me that we never had any sexual instruction from Mother as teenagers.

According to Olive, there were lots of medical books in our house that she encouraged us to read, but "she never told us not to sleep around, or how, where or with whom to do it." I thought we had lots of sexual instruction. In my mother's uniquely obscure way, it was contained in a single sentence, learned in her girlhood and passed on to my sisters and me: "The purpose of intercourse is procreation."

In a sense Olive was correct. Telling your daughters not to sleep around would be, in my mother's opinion, like telling your kids not to put beans up their noses. Why give them any ideas? For my mother, there was a beauty and utility to generic instructions. When she taught her daughters in her simple statement to make love only when they wanted to have babies, she thought they could figure out where and with whom. She also expected we could find books on "how," as she had.

Of course, the sex education of her adolescent daughters lay far in the future on the day my mother mailed my father an obscure postcard before she went to work at the hospital. But she had chosen the sower for the next generation. She wrote:

> There is a minute before duty. From the rich yields of the past we garner hope for the future. I trust none too much my good sower were I to trust everything. It is not possible to do more than sort out the best of what we still have and sowing what we chose, make sure of tomorrow's harvest.

THIRTEEN

At Least Three Women in a Lather

I have to stop writing so many women and monkeying
    around. . . .
I must pull myself together and not be content to receive
    and
Write letters and talk to Hoboes and make speeches to
    students.
I have to get on an economic and spiritual foundation.
                        —*Ben Reitman to Eileen O'Connor, 1934*

After his weekend in Detroit with Eileen O'Connor, my father now had an unpaid secretary and possible coauthor for his new project. He sent Eileen back to Buffalo with outlines and clippings that she was to work on independently. They planned for her to leave Buffalo as soon as her employer could spare her. Ben's idea was that he would provide the raw material of his experience, and Eileen would write the manuscript. He also expected her to handle his daily mail, including his letters from other women.

Now that the book was in good hands, Ben returned to his usual full schedule. In addition to his patients and correspondence, there were his other activities. "I have been so crowded with visitors that I was unable to work much," he wrote Eileen. "That is one of the things you will save me from. I am booked to speak Sat. & debate Sunday also to talk at the unemployed Council soon. I forgot the date." Also on his mind was "Margaret" (Eileen's middle name and now a pet name for her vagina). He wrote, "Glad that Margaret is recovering. Tell her she has to be prepared for heavy work. The next 15 years she will have a daily task."

Eileen's social status in Chicago as Ben's mistress, and the possibility that word of this might get back to Buffalo, was clearly spelled out by Ben, although he still held out hope that Rose would divorce him. He wrote:

> I am so sorry to have to say all this love, but we must face
> All issues. And if you are to survive beautifully
> You must have more than an ordinary love for me, much
>   more
> Than a secretary's interest in "Living with Social Outcasts."
> Did you ever realize Lover, that YOU ARE ABOUT TO LIVE
>   WITH OUTCASTS.
> And do you know that YOU may become a Social Outcast.

Ben and Eileen's book was doomed from the beginning. In contrast to the straightforward outline in his first letter to Eileen, his expectations were, by now, hopelessly grandiose. The book had become "a call to Duty, a pilgrimage to SAVE OUR SOULS/ to Unite all souls to establish a new RELIGION, and to unite all men." Even Ben acknowledged that he was out of touch with reality in his enthusiasm for the new book. "We have to be mighty careful who hears us talk this way," he wrote. "I suppose you know I have what might be termed a Messianic Complex."

After six weeks of correspondence, Ben also revised his earlier opinion of what Eileen could contribute. He now saw his coauthor's strengths to be the "mind and sensibility of a typical book buyer." He wrote, "You are not an intellectual or overly smart, but you have kept your feet on the ground, your heart pure and your mind open." Unfortunately, Eileen's writing experience consisted of dictated medical reports, her own letters, and some poems including one entitled "Lovers Lane Just for Two."

Eileen lived in Ben's apartment along with Ida and Brutus for several months in the summer of 1933 while she and Ben worked on the manuscript. Predictably, Ida behaved as jealously as she had with Eileen's predecessors. Ben kept his other correspondents posted on his activities. Rose was bitter that Ben had driven to Buffalo to pick up Eileen without stopping to see her in New York. Medina wrote Ben, "I hope your new secretary is all you are looking for and she can even compare with the total of the five the previous week."

Surprisingly, at age forty-five, Eileen became pregnant. She wrote Ben a letter as if from the unborn baby (a technique that he would later use extensively) which said "she" was coming, but Eileen's happiness did not last long. When the completed manuscript was rejected by the publisher, Ben bitterly accused her of "satiating him with sex and spoiling his book." She miscarried the same day. Grieving the loss of her baby, but still hopeful there could be a future reconciliation with Ben, Eileen left Chicago in September to stay with relatives in Canada.

Eileen and Ben continued to write regularly, with Ben often complaining about his financial troubles. Hoping he would still take her back, Eileen wrote him in November that she would help pay his debts. "We'll even pay off Rose, if a wife must be paid," she added.

Eileen's willingness to help Ben with his debts and to pay off Rose was not shared by Medina. In fact, she encouraged Ben to go back his wife. "It has been my observation tho that love nests have more thorns than the domestic coop and birds in them argue even less harmoniously than those in the regulation barn yard," Medina wrote. "I hope you take the time to consider her [your wife's] point of view and send for her."

Medina also did not take seriously Ben's periodic news about his new lovers. She wrote him at the end of 1933:

I had thought that at your age and experience one woman more or less would hardly keep you awake nights or color your mornings to quite that extent. . . . Women are startlingly similar. The differences that are apparent are largely individual ones. With you it is the last one that counts.

I am just like all the others. I feel like hugging your neck, and kissing you, and making a baby.

By 1934 my father's correspondence had grown so large that I marvel at his ability just to keep track of the recipients. At his peak he was writing almost daily letters to Medina and Eileen (when Eileen was not in Chicago), and occasional letters to former and current lovers, friends, his wife Rose, professional and political colleagues, and to prisoners, patients, or strangers who had requested his help.

Unexpectedly, after such a long silence, one of his more regular correspondents during this period was Emma. She had arrived in Canada in December and was awaiting final visa clearance for a ninety-day American tour, her first since her deportation in 1919. Despite Ben's repeated suggestions that they reestablish their former relationship and that he manage her tour, Emma refused. In what is probably the best description of my father's flaws as well as his power, she wrote him from Toronto:

You certainly have not changed. Both in your violent moods and those that used to soothe my ruffled spirit, you have remained the same. No one could beat you in your capacity for wounding those who loved you. Or hypnotising them by your capacity to cajole, plead and abase yourself to make one set aside one's hurt. No, you have not changed. Only your appeal has lost its force. At least to me. . . . For a moment it seemed as if we had never been torn asunder with years of pain between us. But it was a rude awakening, the awakening to reality. . . . The struggle to overcome the past has taken more than half the years since you had gone the way of all flesh. It had been very bitter indeed. I could not face another dose. I feel I owed you this frank admission. . . . Let us be friends and meet as such when the time comes. It will save us both much heartache.

Not long afterwards, my father did exactly what Emma had described. After reviewing his major sins as she had described them in her autobiography—his cowardice in San Diego, his short-changing of the book fund, his desertion of her when the war was on, his womanizing—he offered his "tearless sobs" at her rejection. "But whether true or not," he wrote, "I shall reach out my arms for you and say, as I often did, 'Where can I go and hide? What's left for me to do? Oh, God, I loved you, so.'"

In January 1934 Ben's income became more assured when he found a temporary position as a sociologist for a federal study of the homeless men in Chicago's shelter houses. After a five-month separation, Eileen decided to return to Chicago. Ben wrote to her about his new position and her future with him:

Dear Eileen, you gave me too much you sacrificed too
    willingly
For me to say anything that might hurt you.
I gave you the best that was in me in love and loyalties.
You know how hard we tried to write our book.

But we couldn't make it go, the idea of Living with Social
    Outcasts
Was great and it had the possibilities of success.
But it didn't go. I failed miserably.
Now working with a total stranger I am writing real socio-
    logical literature.

Do you see my dear Friend, what I am trying to say.
Life with me is work, service, economic independence.
I must feel that God is blessing me.
And God didn't bless our work and I sank deeper into
    debt. . . .

Now dear as I said before, if Chicago calls you, come.
I shall always be glad to see you
We have very much in common beside a glorious romance.
I am sure you will find a job, a home and expression.

While she was looking for permanent employment in Chicago, Eileen worked for Ben, accepting payment only out of necessity. Probably it was her constant presence, along with Emma's lack of interest, that encouraged Ben to try to improve his relations with his wife. I'm sure Ben read Eileen his letters to and from Rose as she was working in his office. Not content with inviting Rose back, Ben wrote to Emma, "You will have to be careful when you get to Chicago. You know when I make up my mind to seduce a woman what happens. And I have my heart all set on winning you." My mother wrote him later, "You are never happy unless you have at least three women in a lather."

Ben's attempts at seduction were the least of Emma's worries. She had written to a friend earlier, "I don't care for a resurrection of my past with Ben. But I dare say he would make a rousing material success of my tour. But I have learned that one does not live by bread alone." Emma's premonition that her tour would not be a financial success was correct. With the exceptions of New York, Rochester, and Chicago, the tour was so unsuccessful that Emma had to ask friends to pay her living expenses.

In March, after years of reluctance to leave his large apartment by the lake, economic necessity finally forced Ben and his mother and son to move to the small cottage that he owned on the South Side. Emma arrived in Chicago a few days later. Ben and other comrades of Emma's provided additional publicity and arranged for a lower price of admission to her lectures to encourage attendance. She considered it her most successful stop. After Emma left Chicago, Ben wrote her frequently until a final letter from her ("the best and most understanding letter you have written me in 15 years") appeared to satisfy him. Emma could afford to be in a generous mood. At sixty-five, she had found a new love in Chicago: a thirty-six-year-old blind graduate student.

With Emma gone and Ben's mother "still guarding me from Women," he could again focus on his writing. In addition to the reports on the shelter-house men which he hoped to make into a book, Ben also had an offer from Lippincott to publish a book on women hoboes and radicals with the option that it might be done as an "autobiographical" novel.

Eileen tried hard to find work in Chicago and to reestablish her relationship with Ben during this period, but she was unsuccessful in both areas. Ben wrote to a friend:

> Different vibrations, pathological chemistry is in my blood. Last year in April I was under the magic spell of the Irish Queen. This April she is a load on my soul. Last month the Doctor thrilled me, this month I was indifferent. Someday I'm going to work on the Chemistry of moods."

By sometime in April, Eileen could no longer deny Ben's rejection or afford to stay in Chicago without permanent employment. Before leaving for Buffalo, she wrote him:

> I've been so stubborn, so determined, so sure I was right. It's true I did think God did tell me what to do. I stayed only this week hoping I'd get some money—and am so ashamed it doesn't come. . . . You can't hide your great white shining

soul from me and you've been so hurt and hurt through the years.

Now depressed and ill, Eileen stayed with her family, but her correspondence with Ben continued in the same forgiving and apologetic vein.

In the spring, before my father left for New York to spend two weeks with Rose, he made arrangements to see my mother while he was there. After Ben's return from what he wrote Eileen were "the two most perfect weeks of his life," Rose went to the hospital where Medina worked to confront her. Medina sent him the following telegram:

> This afternoon while I was juggling a pan of water in each hand and a bed pan on the chest a well behaved looking brown eyed woman came up and asked me if I were Medina Oliver. I admitted the name. She said she supposed I knew who she was. She seemed a little insistent and irritating but I assured her I had no idea. In a most melodramatic tone she said I am the little plain Jewish wife. My mind was so far from Rose. She seemed more lenient after she saw my noble work. I explained that I could not talk with her there so she insisted that I come to her place tomorrow evening. She was a little abusive when she spoke of you. I have no particular desire to go to her house but if I could mollify her I would make the effort. She sounded a bit dippy. Wire me yes or no and your blessings.

I do not know what my father replied, but my mother did talk with Rose after this incident and, according to my mother's later letter to Ben, gave "her word to Rose that she will bend her efforts toward seeing Rose's marriage through ten years." Whether my mother deliberately lied to Rose to get rid of her, or whether she thought the current arrangement could be stable until Ben himself initiated the break from

Rose, I do not know. When I knew her, my mother's style was rarely confrontational—particularly, I am sure, when dealing with a hysterical or "dippy" stranger. Ben's marriage was a subject on which my mother was probably not clear herself. Although she wanted Ben to choose her over Rose, my mother did not want to acknowledge that she was trying to undermine his marriage.

After her meeting with Rose, essentially nothing changed in Medina's letters. She continued to write several times a week encouraging Ben in his health and writing, and discouraging his politics and habit of borrowing money.

Eileen and Ben had also been corresponding continuously, including one letter in which he told her Medina might be pregnant. Eileen's sweetness finally broke. She wrote to Ben:

> How dare you suggest I am one of your outcasts or a discarded sweetheart? I am not an outcast. I can return to Buffalo Community Hospital immediately at a good salary in a good position. (You didn't take me away from there. I took myself and it was a good thing.) . . . Now on June 18th or 19th I'm leaving to take up life in a new city. You don't need me or want me. It's shameful and unkind of you to treat me like a little begging outcast. It's unfair and unjust of you. Just forget me. Leave me alone.
>
> You say you'll never let me go. You let me go the minute I lost your baby and I've been gone ever since only I didn't realize it. Now you've the hope of another baby and books and jobs. Just let me go on my way alone where I belong.

But one week later, Eileen could not help adding her new address in Cleveland to her "final" good-bye letter.

Within a month Ben asked Eileen to come back to Chicago. He had accepted a $400 advance from his publisher to write an novel about a woman hobo and needed a secretary.

Eileen returned, still hopeful that Ben's need for her might be permanent. This time, she was able to find a full-time position in Chicago as a hospital secretary, and could afford to devote the rest of her time to helping Ben with his projects on a voluntary basis. Over the next year Eileen also "loaned" Ben $600 from her savings, almost half of her annual salary. Ben would later refer to the money in his letters to Eileen, making the figure even higher, and express his regrets at his inability to pay her back.

Despite my mother's promise to Rose, the power of my father's attraction remained as strong as ever. "I know what I want to do with the force that pulls me to you," she wrote him. "I want to live with you; to make children; to raise them. . . . I want some half Jewish children to raise even if it is against all of the laws of the prophets. I hope and believe in that variety."

Medina could handle Rose's self-righteous claims to Ben, as long as he did not agree. But like Eileen's experience with Ben a few months earlier, the turning point came when he invited Rose to spend her summer vacation in Chicago. After Rose had been in Chicago for several weeks, Ben wrote Medina that he was "more in love with my wife now than ever before because she brings me peace and a desire to write." He ended the letter, "All this may be but a mood, but nevertheless I have it in my mind to say it and so I say it. Tomorrow I may be different and be longing for some other woman, but sufficient to the day is the evil thereof."

My father's estimate of the time it would take to change his mind was accurate. Although Eileen and Rose were both in Chicago, within a week he wrote Medina offering to have an affair over her vacation in September if she would help him with his book. But this time my mother could no longer respond in the same way. Turning down his offer, she wrote him:

A novel appears as ridiculous for you as a role in a Broadway burlesque for me would be. I studied dancing five years; I do not dance. You studied spelling fifty years; you do not spell. Your sentences have no particular construction and are rarely units in thought or structure. You have heard of the paragraph, but the accompanying indentation is made by the stenographer. Sequence and organization are yours should chance happen to mother them. Even if you promise to turn from haste and hash to the delicacy of deliberation, I would be unfit to help you with any sort of novel from the dime store kind far past the four hundred dollar variety. . . . It is rare for the horse that pulls the plough to be able to race. If you want to trot with a 2 wheeler for 400 dollars, I would be the last to try and stop you.

However, as their correspondence continued, my mother could gradually feel herself succumbing to "womanly surrender" in response to my father's letters. As Eileen had done earlier, she now wrote one last bitter letter in which she considered that Rose could be paid off to relinquish Ben, if she were so inclined. But, unlike Eileen, she also suggested that money could buy my father's love as well. Speaking of herself in the third person, my mother wrote:

Medina has money; very little in terms of New York of course. . . . For $5,000 she could salve Rose's grief and with $10,000 effect a cure—money. There is so little of grief that one feels like purchasing. . . . Mr. Rockefeller [benefactor to the nursing program] gives Medina $55.25 per month for the opportunity for work and health. One-tenth is not too much to give for love. The Bible says to give one-tenth. Ben can take a ten dollar bill out of his pocket when he feels depressed and change his mood.

Finally, she decided that Ben was worth any emotional

and financial price she had to pay, even if it meant she would be hurt by him repeatedly. She wrote him, "Even in these perilous economic times and with the fear of repetition gnawing at my vitals, it is the right time for me to multiply; it is the right time for a modicum of happiness." She agreed to meet him in Pittsburgh for the weekend to help him "deliver" the "pregnancy" of his new book.

Six months later, after a happier second meeting in Pittsburgh with Ben, my mother would be able to recall her guilty feelings about Rose and her sense of isolation that weekend. But on her return to New York this time, she was conscious only of her happiness at being back with Ben and the thought of spending her vacation with him in September. She wrote him:

> I love you. I want to be with you. I think I could be better to you and better for you than eight women per day. Next to being with you, I enjoy your letters. I adore hearing from you. I haven't felt cross or unhappy or disturbed over you. I remember the times we were together as happy ones—as extraordinary happy ones so far.

Eileen would write Ben a similar letter two months later when he was back in New York conferring with his publisher, living in Rose's apartment, and also seeing Medina. By accident, Eileen surprised Ben in a compromising situation with a young woman in his office a few days before his departure. He came to her rooming house that evening to apologize "with tears in his eyes." As she reviewed the story to him:

> You were in such pain and hurt when you came last Sunday. My God, my Ben, what is there in me that causes you to do that? I tell you truly I never have any visualization of you with anyone else. I mean it—it may be supreme arrogance but I feel it's just true that our relationship is all that concerns me.

Like my mother, Eileen could imagine her love story with Ben with herself as the heroine.

What contribution Rose made to Ben's inspiration or writing is unknown, but two letters she wrote to him, which he sent on to my mother, illustrate the hazards of making Ben "the vase that held my hopes." After he left New York in October, Rose wrote:

> It is self evident that you could not write while you were here—You were a soul cheat each & every hour. . . . You at least were kindly, agreeable, pleasant—that fully returned itself to you in peace of spirit—But you cheated abominably with your love mail—You give nothing to those Medinas— You take all. . . . My hopes and dreams of working with you on a book—the child of my soul— you've dashed against the stone crags of a N.Y. school house. . . . You, the vase that held my hopes, my dreams, my soul—choked them each & all—what jealousy can I bear? what emotion—except pity at the destructiveness—

Two days later she wrote Ben again, assuring him that her motives for criticizing him were "sane, wise, constructive and aimed at your good," even though the criticism was not well received. She ended the letter by describing herself as a "wife who served the best part of life in a silent adoration—and who in spite of pains untold—still breathes in the air of your presence everywhere."

Rose, Eileen, and Medina were not the only women Ben tried to enlist in helping him with his book about women. Even Emma, still in Canada hoping against odds to be readmitted to the United States, was asked to write a chapter on radical women. Emma refused without hesitation. She wrote, "I can only hope that you will not again grow bitter and charge me with all sorts of dire offenses. As to you writing a chapter about me. Why don't you do it? It ought not to be so difficult."

My father had succeeded in having "three women in a lather," but he was still insatiable. His response to all the women in his life was the following poem. I know he sent copies to Emma and "Jo," an occasional lover and friendly correspondent. No doubt there were others as well.

Servants Sewers and Saviors

I need a new woman to whom I can pour out my soul;
The other women in my life seem incomplete.
They don't seem to be able to reach me or hear my cry.
That's the terror of being a "Big Man;"
You are not supposed to cry, have needs, or be lonely.

Others didn't fail me; they just didn't understand my
   language.
They didn't realize how much loving and encouragement an
   "Artist" needs.
The ten years I was with that Giant of All Women Propa-
   gandists
I spent serving her and thinking of her needs.
She climbed high on my shoulders.
The decade I was with my son Brutus's Mother
I climbed, did an enormous amount of work
I rose on her shoulders but sapped her precious life blood.
But that is the only way "God's Work" is done.

All big souls have an enormous capacity.
They need flesh, obstacle, blood, enemies, service, goals.
And that's the pathos of life—we haven't developed
A type of man and woman who can get joy out of serving
   and loving;
Women don't want anyone to stand on their shoulders, or
   get ahead of them

They all want to stand on their own feet . . . and face the sun.
There never can be great souls unless they are willing to be
  foundations. . . .

I am in the market for a pound of flesh. . . .
The pay I offer is suffering for those who have a Christian
  conscience;
Frustration for those who have personal ambition
Life—the abundant life for her who can mount a star.

I would have to agree with Jo's response to his poem: "It's
the most honest and shameless expression of your philosophy
I've ever seen you make."

FOURTEEN

Medina is the Promised Land

There is nothing to feel bad about.
Your parents have you with them.
I want you to be LOYAL to your family and your
      people. . . .
Try living at home at 30, see what kind of adjustment
      you can make.
Maybe you belong to TEXAS.

—Ben Reitman to Medina Oliver, 1935

After graduating from nursing school in the summer of 1934, my mother took a nursing position at New York Hospital and enrolled in nearby Columbia University as a graduate student in bacteriology. In addition to her own work, she planned to help Ben rework his novel about his hobo heroine, Box Car Bertha, through what they thought would be its final stages.

Medina's growing reservations about Ben's project were reflected in her new terminology. She was no longer helping to "deliver" Ben's "pregnancy", the manuscript had become a "fecal increment" that needed treatment before it became a "public nuisance." "If I see any order or sequence in your book I shall take part of the credit," Medina wrote at first. "The beauty is yours." But a month later, she acknowledged the magnitude of the problem. "I'm not able to help you with your work much. Sometimes I think I am more wear and tear on you than anything else, but you are my gasoline."

When Ben submitted the manuscript to the publisher in December, he conceded reluctantly when the publisher wanted it rewritten by a professional writer. He wrote to the publisher, Bert Lippincott:

> If you invest $150 in Ben Reitman making a tour across the country, he could do more for SISTERS OF THE ROAD than if you invested $1,500.00 in the best literary person in America. . . .Don't wait until I'm weary or dead. . . .

> Awake! Thou that sleepest. You've got a chance to sell 50,000 copies of SISTERS OF THE ROAD.

However, Lippincott persisted, and Ben or the publisher arranged for Marjorie Peters, a social worker in Chicago who had been recommended by Nels Anderson, Ben's former student, to rewrite the manuscript. It was a disastrous collaboration. Despite Ben's attempts to interfere with her writing, Peters continued working on the manuscript until the spring of 1936 when a second publisher, Macaulay, bought the rights.

My mother's interpretation of my father's problem with Peters was his inflated assessment of his writing ability. She wrote him:

> Everything that has been a real contribution to the literature has been polished over many, many times. There is some reference in the Bible about the earlier Jews being so inspired that they were able to snatch perfection from the literature directly from Jehovah. Since their time, however, almost all writers have had to toil with diligence.

Anderson commented in a letter to Ben, "Marge believes you have a good story but cold. Box Car Bertha is Ben Reitman and a bit of a lot of women besides. She must be made consistent with female facts. You don't know female

Ritzy New King of Hoboes
Is Frock-Coated and Suave

DR. BEN REITMAN

Dr. Ben Reitman Grants Audience to Press,

Newspaper clipping, no source or date.   *(Ruth and Joel Surgal)*

Earliest photo of Lewis (left) and Ben Reitman   *(Ruth Reitman Highberg)*

My grandmother,
Ida Reitman.
"Ben's passion for her
a menace to his love
for any other woman."
(Rhoda Reitman Kuster)

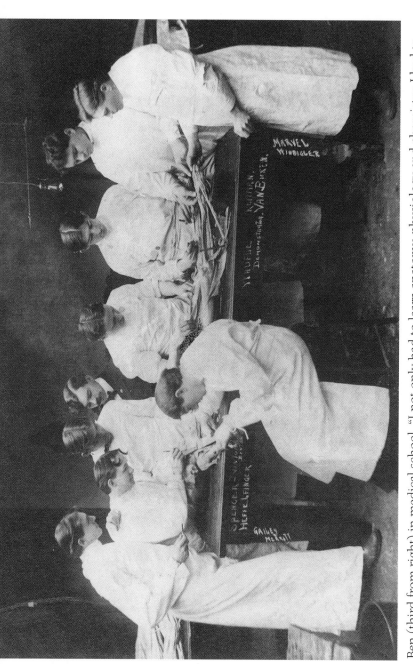

Ben (third from right) in medical school. "I not only had to learn anatomy, physiology and chemistry, I had to learn reading, writing, and arithmetic."

(Reitman Family)

Emma Goldman circa
1910. "Friend and foe
knew her power on
the lecture platform."
(Library of Congress)

Ben Reitman circa 1908.
"He looked a handsome brute."
(Rhoda Reitman Kuster)

MOTHER EARTH

Vol. VII.   JUNE, 1912   No. 4

SAN DIEGO EDITION

PATRIOTISM IN ACTION

Overdrawn but real enough. The night Ben and Emma arrived in
San Diego, Ben was abducted by the vigilantes, beaten, tarred and
sagebrushed and IWW burned on his buttocks with a lit cigar.
(Mother Earth, *June, 1912, Emma Goldman Papers Project, University of
California, Berkeley*)

Ben and comrades advertise Emma's lecture in 19
(Univ. of Illinois at Chicago, The University Library, Dept. of Special Collectio

Ben and Anna Baron in *Mother Earth* office circa 19
(Emma Goldman Papers Project, University of California, Berke

Ben (standing second from left) at the Chicago Hobo College.
(Univ. of Illinois at Chicago, The University Library, Dept. of Special Collections)

Anna Martindale.
Ben and Anna were
together 13 years.
(Ruth and Joel Surgal)

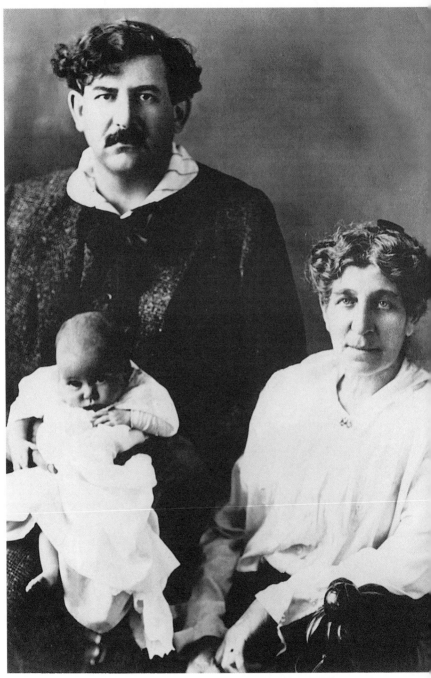

Ben, his son Brutus, and his mother, Ida in 1918.   (Rhoda Reitman Kuster)

Ben's daughter, Helen.
She later changed
her name to Jan Gay.
(*Ruth and Joel Surgal*)

Ben and Brutus.
Estranged from his
daughter, he remained
close to his son.
(*Reitman Family*)

LEARN FROM CUPID

Ben and Rose Siegel Reitman
at their wedding in 1931.
(Newspaper clipping, source unknown.
Univ. of Illinois at Chicago,
The University Library,
Dept. of Special Collections)

My mother
Medina Oliver, 1932
(Reitman Family)

Emma Goldman, 1934.
(UPI/Corbis-Bettman)

Sketches of Ben, 1937.
*(Department of Special Collections,
Phoenix, University of Chicago Library)*

Thought to be Eileen O'Conno
(Univ. of Illinois at Chicago, The University Library, Dept. of Special Collections

My father and me
circa 1940.
(Dorothy Reitman)

...rutus in flight training, circa, 1941.   (*Dorothy Reitman*)

Brutus's widow
Dorothy Reitman
and their son Jan, 1943.
(*Dorothy Reitman*)

HAYMARKET SHRINE OF MEMORY

In November 1942 my father and Eileen O'Connor were the sole participants at a vigil for the Haymarket Martyrs in Waldheim Cemetary (now Forest Home). Ben died a few weeks later.
(Newspaper clipping, source unknown. Univ. of Illinois at Chicago, The University Library, Dept. of Special Collections)

(right) The words of Haymarket Martyr August Spies came true. On May 3, 1998 the Haymarket Martyrs' Monument was designated a National Historic Landmark commemorating the Labor Movement's struggle for worker's rights.
(From a poster by Oscar William Neebe, III, copyright the Illinois Labor History Society)

THE DAY WILL COME...

SHOW THE WORLD
THAT LABOR IS STRONG
AND MOVING FORWARD

GATHER AT THE
HAYMARKET MARTYRS' MONUMENT
AND CELEBRATE ITS DESIGNATION:

NATIONAL HISTORIC LANDMARK

SUNDAY, MAY 3, 1998 - 2 P.M.

FOREST HOME CEMETERY
863 DESPLAINES AVENUE
FOREST PARK, ILLINOIS

...When our silence will be more powerful than the voices you are throttling today.

August Spies
Haymarket Martyr

This was the only father I knew as a child:
old, pensive, and loving and devoted to my mother.
(*Reitman Family*)

facts because your researches stop too low down and end too soon afterwards." Peter's side of the story can be inferred from Ben's letter to Lippincott more than a year later: "I think she mentioned it to you that she could not work with me because I insisted on being intimate with her. I never deny anything *** I hope to tell that story someday."

Once the manuscript was out of Ben's hands, he was free to plan his next book, a rebuttal to Emma's *Living My Life*, and to find fault with Medina. The book on Emma did not materialize because Emma refused to release her letters for publication. "You are much younger, dear Ben and you will outlive me," Emma wrote. "Is it asking too much to wait until then? I do not want my letters to you published, not the part dealing with the struggle of my love for you. It was entirely too dominant, too elemental and too all-absorbing to make it common property during my lifetime."

Medina, now concerned that "women who have never borne children frequently reach the menopause early," refused to be discouraged. "Ben honey!" she wrote, "Your suggestion that I should stop writing you is a well thought out one. There are those capable of saying I should never have begun. There is no truly easy way of stopping me. Sympathy, exposure, ridicule and other methods seem so useless. I feel sure I shall manage to run down as it were of my own accord after a little more time."

Neither her graduate work in bacteriology at Columbia nor her work at New York Hospital held Medina's interest long, and she decided to return to her family in Texas in the spring of 1935. Brutus left for a hobo tour of Europe after finishing high school in midyear, and Ben decided to make a cross-country tour by car while his son was gone. He offered to drive Medina from Chicago to her parents' house in Houston. Both of them remembered the week on the road as a particularly happy time together.

My father's stay in Houston was brief. In addition to his

soapbox efforts to introduce my politically and fiscally conservative grandparents to anarchism, he also claimed that he had lost his money en route and asked them for a replacement "loan." Although polite, their dislike for him was obvious. After my father's departure, my mother wrote him of her parents' reaction, possibly expressing her own doubts as well:

> I feel so helpless where you are concerned. I love you, honey, but I am not able to make my folks feel kindly and gracious or even hospitable toward you. . . . There is nothing ugly or vicious or mean about you that I have ever seen. You are a sweet old panhandler but that isn't your fault altogether. My family see you as a person lacking in morals and principles. They picture you in as ugly and sordid a light as Rose would picture me to the nuns. Rose thinks of me as a grasping vampirish person; they think of you as an exploiter, as a person to use my feeble mindedness to bad ends. All seem silly and lacking in truth. Real truth is elusive and difficult to find however.

On his return to Chicago, the desperate state of his finances encouraged my father to perform abortions despite their illegality. He wrote of his reservations to Brutus: "I want to get away from paying my rent with the hard earned dollars of women who love passionately but without a knowledge of birth control." The abortions alarmed my mother. Generally critical of Ben's skill as physician, she worried that his ineptitude would kill a patient, not an uncommon occurrence in the days before antibiotics. She wrote, "Your description of your abortion grinds my soul, Ben. . . . I pray that the little pimpled gal will live, if she still wants to and she most probably does. . . . To lay a woman liable to . . . infection is more than defying the order of things; it seems like a taunt."

Medina was still mulling over her future as an unmarried woman who wanted children. She wrote:

I wish it were possible to describe the mental processes of a woman born to be an old maid who sleeps with a man. I am sure it must seem self deception, the assumption of a feeling of trust, and partial hypnotism. . . . Of course, yours and my love is different. Conceived in heaven, born on the sidewalk of Maxwell Street, nurtured in the most out-of-the-way places; there is no telling what may become of it. Certainly I should feel too old to be hanging around the altar hoping all may end in marriage. Up to now, my hope has been in procreation, but should you consider remaining permanently in the abortion business, I contemplate giving even that hope away.

Ben's reply was hardly reassuring. He wrote, "Business continues very slow. There is absolutely no danger that I might become an Abortionist or a Dope peddlar. I can go without things with very little trouble. And so far I have always been able to borrow when I was in need."

Unable to find work and unhappy with her life at home, Medina had only one outlet: her letters to Ben. But Ben was not content with sending only his letters. He persisted in sending her Rose's letters as well. After receiving one letter, Medina replied:

I am unable to stomach Jewish bitterness; your feelings for your crown of thorns; for the nails in your palms I find obnoxious. One of your race went through all that once. . . . When you and Rose crucify, you have no purpose. . . . Keep her letters and please do not add to her unhappiness by throwing the letters I write you into her path.

You are mistaken when you assume that your summer amours affect me. I am farther from you than I have ever been.

My father's reply is one of my favorite letters. It illustrates why both my father and my mother could not stop writing. For my mother, writing Ben was "the most fun" she had. For both of them it was a way of thinking about themselves and the world. My father wrote:

> Other people's letters that I send and many of my own bother you.
> Can't you see that is unimportant.
> Just as unimportant as if you are "farther away from me than ever before". . . .
> How many times must I tell you I WRITE YOU BECAUSE in writing you
> I make things plain to my self.
>
> Don't you suppose if there were Gods and they could listen to their people
> Praying to them, and they would see all of the stupidity and selfishness of the
> Prayers they would feel like spitting in their eyes or voiding on them.
> Yes I see how ridiculous and selfish I am appearing to you.
> And I clearly comprehend your lack of interest in all that I do.
> But that doesn't stop me or bother me at all. If I could get direct to God.
> I would not bother with you. In the mean time you will have to stand for me.

In August a position as a nursing instructor and laboratory supervisor opened in the nursing school of Sparrow Hospital in Lansing, Michigan. My mother left for Lansing immediately, stopping in Chicago on the way. While she was with Ben, he received a phone call from another woman. My mother wrote him after her arrival in Lansing, "I will always remember your telephone conversation during this last visit. Not that anything matters particularly. I only want to be the last. You won't deny me the opportunity of coming after the others have gotten through with you. I have tried to learn to be useful."

Ben, now contrite about his previous behavior, comforted Medina during her transition to the new job. He wrote, "Darling I don't want to get on your nerves and shall only answer your letters. I promise you I will not bother you with my poems or letters of friends. I am yours." Ben also expressed his change in feelings in a letter to his eighteen-year-old son, "I pine and long for Medina like a sick calf, but my bowels seem to move and there are others. But Medina is the PROMISED LAND."

Being less than 250 miles apart made it feasible for my mother and father to see each other more often, and any doubts about Ben that she felt while living with her family now evaporated. Medina's stay in Michigan was characterized by Ben's most consistently loving behavior thus far. Years later, in my mother's reminiscences to my sisters and me, this was the time she referred to as her "courtship."

Besides proximity, their relationship was aided by her lack of competition. Ben's persistent "borrowing" from his friends and lovers had a predictably chilling effect on his social life. Jo, who had been Ben's lover for several years, was typical. "I'm still fond of you and interested in you," she wrote him that summer. "But I don't feel like sleeping with you anymore. You are too heavy a load for me to carry."

Medina continued to be critical about Ben's shortcomings, particularly his begging and giving away money. Undaunted, he responded that he needed her, but not to the point of reforming. He wrote:

You "have my number." I like most of the people who have
   come into my

Office for help, need very little help and any money that is
   given or loaned me
Is worse than wasted.
Since I saw you I gave Coxey enough money to almost pay
   my rent.
He would have gotten along as well without it.
The last half dozen men that were in my office for a touch
   this week
Spent it mostly on booze.
NEVERTHELESS . . . the next half dozen or next thousand
   men or men who ask me
Will receive. I hope I can stop asking or hinting BUT I shall
   not stop giving.
"Such as I have I give unto thee."
To give is a weakness, an inferiority complex, a bad habit.
But I shall continue to do it as long as I am able.
And I advise everyone never to give to me or anybody else.

Ben often saw "General" Jacob Coxey in his office. The
former leader of "Coxey's Army," a march of unemployed men
on Washington in 1884, was now a frequent recipient of Ben's
handouts. Ben wrote his friends, "Gen. Coxey . . . made a
great talk at the Theological Seminary Monday and received
ten dollars. Yesterday he asked for the address of a Massage
parlor. Think of it, at 82 spending his last pennies to buy the
touch of a woman. He who has been rich and had a wife and
sweethearts** now he must buy."
   Medina often sent Ben money but she preferred that it go
for special purposes. In a letter written after a visit to Chicago,
she enclosed a check for a new suit and added, "Under separate cover, I am writing your mother about the garments I
forgot. Do not burden Freud with the reason. Try to find my
other shoe buckle and do not give my pajamas to the next one
who comes along."
   She also sent money occasionally on general principles.

She wrote in another letter:

> Consider this two dollars an expression of my love. If I loved you more I would pay your gas bill, your telephone bill, your rent, your paper, postage, and typewriter bill, the rent of your poor improvident dispossessed neighbor, and everything else. I shall never love anybody that much, however. . . . You may be sick but you are not helpless. I would rather you would not write than to have you mention in three successive letters that you owe thirty or forty dollars for gas.

Fortunately, Medina thought Ben's irritating letters were balanced by his more amusing or inspiring ones. "Every so often you write me something so tremendously revealing it repays me a thousand times over for reading the pure 'bunk' that you are also capable of writing," she wrote.

Although Medina and Eileen were not the only women to give Ben money, they gave more consistently, and did not ask for its return. When Ben "borrowed" thirty dollars from June, a former lover now on public relief, he originally had no intention of paying her back. "It is better that she suffer with me than I be a crook to get money," he wrote in a letter, with a carbon copy to June. Not surprisingly, June was indifferent to how he earned the money. He enclosed a note with his repayment: "You did just as I foresaw. Sorry I bothered you. Kindly Ben."

Eileen's awareness of Ben's growing relationship with Medina encouraged her to accept an unusual opportunity while Medina was still in Texas. A mutual friend of Eileen's and Ben's, Adolph Deutsch, was opening a handwriting analysis and natural-foods business on The Pike, an amusement pier in Long Beach, California. He invited Eileen to assist in the business, and to help him write a book on radical politics and pacifism. Although she was promised little more than room

and board, Eileen and Adolph envisioned the business growing to the point that it could support Ben's move to California.

Once she was settled in Long Beach, Eileen and Ben wrote
each other frequently, and Ben periodically sent her his handwritten material to revise and type. Although she consistently
denied any jealousy of "the little snip" (Medina), Eileen's
letters clearly showed her feelings about her rival. "I am glad
you want to sleep in my arms for I assume it's my arms you
mean, though the letter is addressed to 'My Dear Medina!!!,'"
Eileen wrote Ben. "For God knows I want to sleep in yours
whether you want to sleep in Medina's or not."

Reading my father's letters fifty years later, I see his indifference and cruelty to Eileen, but I think she perceived him as
both the affectionate father and the child she never had. She
frequently addressed her letters to Ben as "Dear Daddy" and
also referred to Ben as her "baby" on a number of occasions.
Eileen expressed the sadness of her own and her mother's life
in one of her letters:

> I have never had a home. And I have always wanted a home.
> My earliest recollections are of my mother begging my father
> not to touch her!!! And his voice always raised in fault
> finding with all of us. I know now that he was sick and
> perhaps in his wrong atmosphere. I have felt at home with
> you but always realized that it was that great gift of yours of
> giving yourself to everybody. When I get my little place
> started that will be MY HOME and to it you can come when
> you will and SHARE MY HOME. This gives me a certain
> peace to contemplate.

Eileen often wrote of how she visualized Ben coming to be
with her in California. She slept with his blue scarf on her
pillow to remind her that they would soon be reunited.

It was during her stay in California that Eileen first began
working on Ben's biography, which she tentatively titled, "I

Love Ben Reitman." "My greatness must develop in its hidden current, alone and unsung but when the greatness of some others is written across the skies, my aura will be seen outlining it," she wrote Ben. Eileen believed that the true story about Ben could not be written until after his death. "The spirit of it all is only in my soul and I know I shall get it on paper when the time comes. Your story will never be finished, of course, but I feel there'll be a time when *I'll* be satisfied with it."

The long separation and the opportunity to express herself in her letters also allowed Eileen to gradually acknowledge her bitter feelings towards Ben she had denied earlier. She particularly grieved for her childlessness, blaming Ben for her miscarriage. On a painful anniversary, she even suggested that she could provide Ben with a baby through Medina:

> Two years ago today I lost my little baby—on that day you came to me early in the morning and you said, "You have ruined my book; you have satiated me with sex." The bitter loathing—so that I knew you did not want my baby—your baby. And have I not bled ever since—can I stop bleeding? I've bled literally—every month, so that I'm often rather weak. And daily I'm tortured by my failure, and I tell you I'll never rest till I get you a baby if I have to write Medina myself and drag her here. . . . The ocean is so blue—come to it; I will go if we can't get along, but I think we can—all of us.

Ben's letters continued to assure Eileen that they would be together again soon. A year after Eileen's arrival in California, he wrote her prophetically, "I never have the slightest doubt but that we shall be much together the rest of my life."

Eileen was prepared to make it happen. She had written Ben earlier, "Chance brought me to you but it was me—I— My Character—Determination—whatever you will—kept me here. I was born and lived and grew all to this end."

By the time Rose filed for a legal separation at the end of 1935, Ben's contact with his wife had dwindled to occasional letters. Possibly her suicide threat to Ben the following month was prompted by remorse. There was one more exchange about divorce, but, predictably, Rose would not agree to Ben's unfavorable terms. Although Rose sent Ben periodic invitations to join her on her vacations, they would not see each other again for nearly five years.

Ben's next writing project was a total revision of the autobiography he had started in the 1920s. This time he enlisted the help of Theodore Schroeder, author, psychologist, lawyer, civil libertarian, and Ben's friend since the time of his free speech battle days with Emma. Medina cautioned Ben:

> Your plans are large as usual. Forgive me for any admonitions I might utter. It is my hope that when you get so far as the actual writing, there may be a few items concerning the history of the radical movement and the growth of Chicago as a city which you may be persuaded to leave out; also, that you may fail to mention having slept with all of the figures of the anarchist movement of your time. It might be well to confine yourself to the time when you were awake and in possession of your faculties.

Schroeder lived on the East Coast, and despite their plans, the two men were unable to meet before Ben was hired by the Chicago Board of Health in early 1937. Schroeder remained fascinated with the subject, however, and later attempted to write his own psychological study of Ben, corresponding with Ben extensively in 1942. Ben's death that year terminated the project.

Ben also wrote Emma asking for help with his new version of his autobiography. Emma replied that she would gladly read the manuscript, "and give you my frank and sympathetic opinion." Referring to their arguments over her autobiography, she added, "Do you think you will be able to rise to that without any of your old suspicion that I want to hurt you in any way?"

This was one of Emma's last letters to Ben prior to her silence during her intense involvement with the Spanish Civil War. Following a debilitating and painful illness, Berkman had committed suicide in June 1936. Emma's devastating loss of her comrade of forty-seven years aroused her interest in embracing a new revolutionary cause. After writing to Ben, asking him to publicize Berkman's death, she did not reopen her correspondence until her return to Canada in 1939.

With Emma in Europe, Eileen in California, and Rose in New York, the woman waiting "until the others have gotten through with you" now had her opportunity. After visiting Ben in Chicago, Medina sent the following message:

> If you want to be famous, go right ahead. I want to be happy; to keep as healthy as I can; and to do things. I love to do things. Even the simplest little things like trimming your moustache or cutting your hair make me very happy. I enjoy washing my clothes. If only I had a couple of babies to wash for most likely I could be happy a much bigger percentage of the time.

> Truly if I am not with child now there is very little hope for me. In a few days I'll be writing you whether or no. I feel first rate.

My mother's "concentrated hope," as she later defined prayer to my sisters and me, was finally answered. She was pregnant with what she at first thought were twins, "Medina on the left and Mecca on the right." Playing off her own name, she chose the names of the two cities in Saudi Arabia that are shrines in the Islamic religion. As first-born, I got the name of the Prophet Mohammed's birthplace.

Four years of waiting would seem long enough to develop a strategy, but my mother had none for breaking the news to her family. She operated intuitively on a day-to-day basis. She wrote my father that spring, "Things are sure to go right but when and how is something to predicate. We love each other. My family will not be ugly to you, if they can be made to understand just that."

FIFTEEN

It is All So Delightful, So Interesting

The beautiful thing about life is something is always happening.

—*Ben Reitman to Herbert Blumer, 1936*

Like all the other women in my father's life, my favorite of his love stories is how he came to fall in love with me. My mother's efforts to make a place in my father's life for herself and me, despite all obstacles, amazes me still. Typical of my father, it is also the story of how he helped not one, but two, women to get exactly what they wanted.

Things did not look promising for my future family life in the spring of 1936. My mother expected that she would be fired as soon as her pregnancy became obvious. When Ben threatened to leave his practice to go to either California or New York, she encouraged him to stay in Chicago. "I must have some place to work and something to work at after I lose my figure. To keep that place clean during a whole pregnancy would be penance of Herculean proportions."

My mother visited my grandparents in June, but her pregnancy did not show enough to be detected. She told her parents only that she was moving to Chicago and marrying in November. My grandmother Inez Oliver's letters allude calmly to my mother's marriage. Apparently she was satisfied that her thirty-one-year-old daughter was marrying at all, even if it was to someone Inez did not care for.

Ben wrote Rose that summer that he was an expectant

father and asked for a divorce. Whether she believed him or not, she was not interested in the offer. He also wrote Eileen, without telling her that Medina was pregnant, to ask if she would like a baby. Eileen, now forty-eight, replied, "Darling Ben, I'm still menstruating but I'm afraid I'm too old for a baby. Oh, Ben forgive me."

Despite his request for a divorce from Rose and his delight in his impending fatherhood, my father made no plans for my future. Instead, he preferred to minimize his role by referring to my mother as "the Madonna with child" in his letters to his friends and son. He acknowledged that he was the father of Medina Oliver's unborn child "Mecca" in his will written that fall, but he did not make any provision for the mother or baby.

When my mother was five months pregnant, Ben finally broke the news to Eileen. However painful any thought of Medina's hypothetical baby must have been for Eileen, the news of a real baby's impending arrival hurt more. She did not reply for several weeks. Her silence, followed by a special delivery letter (alluded to but not found among Ben's papers), prompted him to write the following letter to Brutus with a copy to Eileen:

> Eileen thinks that because of Medina and her Child that is
>   en route
> That our relationship is or will be different**
> When Berkman met me at 210 E. 13th and Emma Goldman
>   introduced me as her new LOVER
> Berkman and Emma's relationship never changed. When
> Berkman took on Becky, Fitzie, and others their lovers made
>   no difference in their relationship.
>
> For a big 18 year old Son . . . all this may seem immaterial
>   and irrelevant
> And unimportant, but Son you have to learn and to think

about those things.

That is why I am so anxious for you to know about my life and **

It is all so delightful, so interesting.

Ben neglected to mention that Alexander Berkman and Emma were never lovers again, despite their lifetime friendship, but Eileen recognized that her fantasies of reuniting with Ben in California were now over. She told Adolph she was returning to Chicago "for a visit" at the end of the 1936 summer season.

Ben arranged for Eileen to stay in the home of a friend, and she arrived in mid-September. She began a new diary on the day of her arrival, noting that she and Ben spent the night together in a hotel. After a week in Chicago with Ben, she learned that he planned to retrieve his manuscript for *Sister of the Road* from Marjorie Peters, and cashed in her return ticket.

Fifteen months of separation had prepared Eileen to be persistent. After one of Medina's weekends in Chicago, Eileen dreamed "of a pregnant woman—ugly look on face, deformed back it seemed—sticking open knife towards me—Ben's face beside mine." Undiscouraged, she later remarked in her diary, "God tells me to stay near him."

Until she was able to find paid employment, Eileen worked on several projects for Ben, including consolidating his letters from herself, Medina, Rose, Jo, Emma and others for her own future biography of him. She planned to keep these, along with her first letters from Ben, stored in her trunk until Ben's death, possibly "20 years in the future." She had no way of knowing they would lie unread for more than fifty years. A more immediate project, however, was the current book. As soon as the last sections of *Sister of the Road* arrived, Ben and Eileen started on the new revision.

Until her pregnancy became apparent, Medina could easily

deny her sexual relationship with Ben, as she did on at least
one occasion in New York when questioned by her nursing
supervisor. In the 1930s it was acceptable to talk about sex in
educated or bohemian circles, but it was rare for a woman to
be frank about her own sexual activities. An illegitimate child
meant that the woman had openly flaunted social taboos.

The severity of these social pressures was vividly described
by Ben's lover Jo. Although Jo had many lovers, she was
careful to protect her reputation and her scientific career. She
wrote to Ben in 1934:

> I want to do certain work and society will simply sink her
> ugly treacherous teeth in me if she finds I'm not the virtuous
> and discreet old maid she now smiles upon with a sort of
> pity. . . . I love more freely than anyone I know except you,
> and simply not telling the world makes very little difference.
> If I were free in that way I would not be free to do this work.

My mother did not share her thoughts about her situation
or her future with anyone at the hospital where she was
working, or even with my father. Ben wrote to his son and
daughter, "I am expecting the Madonna in town this evening
but as usual have no idea when she will come. She is a great
soul, asks for nothing, keeps her own counsel, never passes
her fears on."

At work, Medina covered her growing abdomen with
gradually larger lab coats to avoid notice as long as possible, a
behavior that Ben later used for his heroine, Box Car Bertha.
Once the comments began, I'm sure they came rapidly from a
variety of sources. A Japanese physician who worked closely
with my mother in the laboratory was so struck by her
stoicism under constant disapproval that one day he knelt
down and kissed the hem of her lab coat.

Many of my father's patients did not share my mother's
point of view. One of his letters vividly portrays those women

along with the "family man" who makes a living by introducing poor and lonely young women to prostitution. After a particularly trying day at the office, Ben wrote:

5:30 P.M.
  . . . Today I saw three Pregnant women. They were laughing hysterically, crying, pleading,
"Save me, save me."
"My husband knows I went out with another man. I have two children with him
And if I have this child he will kick me out and take my children."
***"If I have a child that is not blond with blue eyes it will disgrace him" ***
The third woman said nothing except "Just fix me up, I got one child and that is enough for the present.". . .

7:30 P.M.
Joe the Pimp walked back to the office with me.
"My girl ran away from me, she was one of the best money makers in town.
No I am not driving a cab. I am running for a swell joint. I see a cab driver
And give them cards, and get a commission on the business they send me.
I have two kids, a boy 12, he is the brightest kid in school. . . .
If you get hold of any girls that are strangers and want a job, send them to me.
I will put them in the racket and we will both make some money."

Although Ben did perform abortions, his opportunities for business far outweighed his willingness. Given the frequency of the problems he saw daily, the best he could offer in most cases was sympathy and encouragement. One grateful patient wrote him, "I have not forgot you and never will forget what you done for me. . . . Things are going as they were before. The baby is getting nice and big."

Medina did not consult a physician about her pregnancy, but calculated that the baby would arrive in late December. Contrary to her expectations, her sympathetic supervisor allowed her to continue working until mid-November. She then left Michigan for Chicago, having arranged with Ben to live with him and his family until after the baby was born, when she would be able to find a new job and move on. The few weeks before I was born would be the longest time my father and mother had ever been together continuously.

Toward the end of her pregnancy, my mother began to feel increasingly ill. She also had some serious disagreements with Ben. In a letter written (but never mailed) to help me obtain a copy of my birth certificate when I was twenty-one, my mother summarized her version of my history to the Illinois Bureau of Vital Statistics:

> The record of Mecca Benn Reitman's birth stands as nearly the truth as I was able to say at the time. . . . The father wanted me to be delivered at home by his teacher of obstetrics, a Dr. Bacon. . . . At that time he was old and engaged in delivering horses in Michigan. It was impossible for me to stomach him as well as the idea of my being delivered at home. Also we disagreed about whether to put the baby on a pink or yellow slip. The father was all for calling the baby illegitimate because he thought she would be able to get along better in Illinois. He held many phone calls with social service but I remained adamant that she was as legitimate as possible with the chosen father.

Of course, my mother never directly suggested anything but legitimacy to my sisters and me as we were growing up. She often told us that she and our father had said their "vows" three times: in New York City; in Livingston, Texas; and in Lansing, Michigan. She never explained the nature of these vows, but that seemed romantic to us, and I suppose helped her cope with the issue of our illegitimacy. In an early version of my autobiography, written when I was in high school, I gave her wedding date as 1932, giving me a respectable four years to come along. Probably I based the date on my mother's story that it had taken her and my father four years of trying before she became pregnant.

As a way of telling—yet not telling—us her secret, my mother had several stories about illegitimacy that she enjoyed repeating. In addition to the pink and yellow slip story, which I heard many times without ever trying to question her further or decipher its meaning, she was also fond of quoting one of her medical professors: "There is no such thing as a fatherless child. Some children just have fathers who lack social consciousness." She never commented on its applicability to her own situation.

My father's activities the first week of December compounded the problems of both my mother's ill health and my legal status. It was comparable, he wrote to friends, to the week he had been tortured in San Diego and the week of his trial and conviction for distributing birth control literature in Cleveland.

Rose called Ben on Monday of that week to ask for Medina's address, threatening to contact Medina's parents, and publicize her and Ben's immoral behavior in Houston and Chicago. Ben immediately responded that if she caused any trouble, he would contact the New York Board of Education about her efforts to blackmail him. Apparently, this was enough of a threat to quiet her. On Tuesday, he left for three days in St. Louis, where he testified about his involvement as a go-between at the trial of a woman accused of baby selling.

Feeling ill and undecided about what to do, my mother

wrote my grandparents that her marriage plans had changed. Knowing that she was now living with Ben in Chicago, my grandmother replied, "If you have changed your plans for the future no one here knows anything about what they were originally, so you would not be molested in any way by Madam Grundy [social disapproval]. We'd be awfully glad to see you for the holidays."

What precipitated Medina's decision to leave is a matter of speculation. With Medina and Ida at close quarters, it would have been out of character for Ida not to be insulting, particularly in Ben's absence. Given her situation, my mother might have taken offence at something relatively minor.

Ben returned from St. Louis to spend a busy Friday in his office where "Patients, Poets, Sociologists, Friends, Hoboes and Women were always in." He appeared on a radio talk show in the afternoon, and ended the day by dining and walking with friends. He also had plans to attend opening night of the new term at the Hobo College with Eileen on Saturday, when he would be speaking. None of these activities involved Medina.

Whether her perception of Ben's lack of concern for her and the baby was the key factor or simply the last straw, something triggered my mother's decision to pack her bags and leave. On Saturday morning, she called my father to say only, "Take care of yourself, I don't want you to know where I live."

Not surprisingly for a man who wrote "I will be remembered by my carbons," on Sunday morning Ben wrote a letter with several carbon copies to his friends describing life's complications. That afternoon, he and Brutus began searching the Chicago hospitals my mother was most likely to have chosen, but did not find her. Brutus was worried about Medina's safety, but if Ben was concerned over the next few days, Eileen did not note it in her diary. Eileen and Ben saw each other almost daily working on the revisions to *Sister of the Road* or attending meetings together. Ben mentioned to

Eileen on Monday that Medina had called to say she was okay, but had refused to give her address.

Getting no response to her letter to my mother, my grandmother Inez Oliver anxiously followed up a few days later with a second letter:

> We can imagine terrible things that might happen to one so unsuspecting and trusting as you are. We do not know to what extent you might be imposed on; nor the kind of people you are with. . . . If you are not married or going to be married, I wish you would clear out from there. . . . At any rate, let us know at once what is wrong or I shall be distressed sure enough.

My grandfather added:

> We all make mistakes and the easier way out is to admit it and look around for a toe hole from which to jump. . . . We shall be glad to help you, if you just limber up enough to let us know in simple English just what you need to escape.

After leaving Ben's cottage, Medina moved to her former rooming house near the University of Chicago. Early in the morning of December 8, several weeks earlier than she expected, she began to feel labor pains. When the pains began coming regularly, Medina left a note for her friends, walked to an all-night diner and called a cab to take her to Cook County Hospital.

After I was born, my mother wrote to my father inviting him to come see me and telling him that we were registered under the name of Benn. In addition to the false name of the father she gave on the birth certificate, my mother also gave a false home address. (While she was still in the hospital, she corrected the home address but left the false name.) When my father and Brutus came to the hospital bringing flowers and my mother's mail, they were able to see me through the observation window. Since the hospital did not allow visitors on the maternity ward, for the next eight days my mother's and father's only contact was by mail.

An unmarried mother in a charity ward of a large county hospital was not uncommon. Medina wrote Ben, "There are seventy other women here in a similar position to my own except that I have flowers and oranges and enough money for stamps." She added a few days later:

> Do not be disturbed about giving Mecca or any of my children a legacy. A good mother provides and I shall try to be a good mother. . . . The world is wide and you are free of the responsibility you never assumed. . . . I pray that Mecca may thrive wherever she happens to land. May she be more adaptable than the generation preceding.

My father called the hospital's Social Service department to discuss my mother's case. My mother reported to him that, as a consequence of his call, she was visited by a social worker who insisted that she tell the truth in order to avoid publicity. Apparently my mother did not take this opportunity. My father always assumed that it was the woman from Social Service who contacted my grandparents. However, the details of their letters suggest to me it was my mother who sent them the news.

Medina wrote her parents that she and Ben had gone through a marriage ceremony but that he was unwilling to divorce his wife. She told them that her new name was Benn. Her father replied, questioning the legality of the marriage ceremony, but offering to help her. Her mother wrote the following day:

> If the lie [of the assumed name] can be lived to the letter, it probably will be better for your good name and the baby's; if

the lie is made matter of record as to marriage license and certificate, and birth certificate, he will be freed from a possible charge of adultery and you can escape him with your baby if you wish. He will probably see that you play him safe; and if he is insincere and a demon, he may go on preying on your love for him to bleed you white for gifts and money for his support, never contributing to the support of his child. . . . He just has one more woman of many, in his grasp to contribute to his upkeep. This is what I suspect unless you know differently.

During her week in the hospital, the "insincere demon" repeatedly asked my mother to return to his family. In his last letter he wrote:

Oh my Darling, won't you try and think in terms
Of being part of our family for a while,
Please try and resign yourself to staying with us.
Until Mecca gets to be a big girl
I beg of you to give me the joy of being a real Father and
    Lover.

My mother and I did go home with my father, and several weeks later, my grandparents sent my mother a package and check for Christmas at my father's house. My grandfather asked her to write him "how you wish us to address you, what do you wish us to say to the kin when they ask about you, how your money is holding out, etc." My mother's reply is unknown. Possibly she was too ashamed to do more than acknowledge the gift.

When I was six weeks old, my father began a series of monthly letters to my grandparents, written in my voice, keeping my mother in touch with her family. He wrote in the first letter to "Grandpa Oliver":

Most of the neighborhood is composed of hard working
honest men and women

And they treat us in a most friendly manner, just as they do
any married woman.

Dad's family and intimate friends accept and love us and
think he is lucky.

Mother is getting over her fear and timidity and is so happy
with me and Dad

But mother is talking about leaving me alone all day while
she goes back to work. . . .

I am getting to be a big ten pound girl, six weeks old next
Tuesday.

And this delightful old world is beginning to unfold its
mysteries to me.

And I am looking forward to a long, happy useful and
unashamed life.

I wish I could tell you about my Dad—but now that is unim-
portant.

I trust you and Gran will be well and happy and Mother and
I can make you proud.

Your loving Grand Daughter
Mecca

An hour later:

Mother read the above letter and for the longest time she
couldn't speak.

Mother has always been afraid of you and her Mother—
afraid to speak;

Afraid to think out loud. You never permitted her to give you
her confidence.

And now, when the greatest desire of her life has been realized, she still fears you.

Please may I ask that you give Mecca more understanding
than you gave Medina.

The contrast between my father's description of domestic
life with my mother to the Olivers and to his thirty-one-year-
old daughter Jan is striking, and cautions anyone reading his
letters not to take anything he wrote as the whole story. His
perception shifted with his moods and audience. His letter to
Jan best describes what he admired about my mother, and is
consistent with what he wrote about her for the rest of his life:

It would take a consummate artist to do her [Medina]
justice. She's a typical American Texan, in speech, demeanor
and character. She's a courageous free soul, knowing what
she wants and getting it at all costs. She is not fully emanci-
pated from her Baptist, conservative ancestry, but she has
brains, character and pride, and less than any woman who
has been in my life she is NOT dependent upon me, either
for economic, spiritual or friendly security. . . . Just now I can
say happily we are together, but I would never be surprised
when she picks up and goes her way to wherever her mood
may direct.

The spelling and punctuation in both of these letters are
too good to be Ben's; they were probably typed by Eileen.
Certainly she read them because one entry in her diary ex-
presses her concern about the wisdom of Ben's letters to
Medina's father. Her diary also gives glimpses of how Medina
came to stay with Ben. More important for her, it describes the
birth of Ben's other "baby" in the spring of 1937. This time,
Eileen would be the "mother"—to Box Car Bertha.

Eileen and Ben worked continuously on the revision of *Sister
of the Road* from the time the new publisher returned the last
section of Peters' version in November until it was resub-

mitted at the end of January. In addition to her work on the book, Eileen also encouraged Ben in his negotiations with the Board of Health to start a venereal disease clinic for hoboes. Medina would have nothing to do with either project. Earlier, when Ben had asked her to work with him at the clinic and to pray for Box Car Bertha, she wrote from the hospital:

> I have plenty of time you would think to pray for your brain children. I wish you well with them, of course. My missionary spirit is too weak. . . . Your ability to treat disease does not impress me. You have a remarkable penetration at times and an ability to treat the individual. It would seem most logical that you wash your hands between each one. A place to take a good bath with soap would cure more hoboes of what ails them than bismuth and "neos" [two drugs for syphilis].

When I was born, Eileen commented in her diary about Medina, "great courage, I'm sure. No love." She also noted that May, Ben's first wife, was now out of the mental hospital and had been coming to Ben's office along with other panhandlers. Unlike Medina, Eileen admired Ben's generosity toward May and the "outcasts" who needed his help.

At Christmas, Eileen and Ben attended the traditional dinner for hoboes at the Hobo College. Although Eileen hoped Medina would be moving on soon, she could see Ben becoming more and more taken with me. She wrote: "Ben says I shall see Mecca before she goes. Poor boy—he is so happy and satisfied about her. I pray Medina will allow her to love her Father. For a week now his brown eyes have talked to her and loved her. Oh God—help her to remember if—later on—"

As the days went by and Medina did not leave, Ben's happiness with me caused Eileen to reflect, "Why can't I act when I know—take myself away! Because it's death—I ache so even now with him so near. He loves that child as I knew he would!"

Despite Ben's delight in what Eileen referred to as "the best Christmas and New Year that he ever had and Medina gave it to him!" she was able to write, "He thought of me yesterday, he said and wanted to be with me." She added, "How hurt I have always felt for men in the hands of women who didn't love them."

In mid-January, Medina found a job at Cook County Hospital and told Ben she was leaving. Eileen reported that now even Ben's mother wanted Medina and me to stay. Having been the target of Ida's jealousy, Eileen may have considered Ida's "Aren't we good enough for her?" equivalent to an effusive welcome.

In her loneliness over being excluded from sharing Ben's life with his baby, Eileen treasured any show of intimacy with him. She recorded kisses, sitting on his lap, or having his arm around her. It seems likely that they continued to be lovers whenever the opportunity arose. Eileen perceived that things continued to be rocky in Ben's cottage; she recorded that one of Medina's uncommunicative spells was probably related to a letter she received from Rose. Eileen noted in her diary:

> Medina just plays with Mecca. Washes 30 or 40 pieces of clothes a day—her little baby! I'll never get to see my little Mecca—she won't let me. She set herself against me from the start. . . . In May 1933 I said to myself, "Medina will cause me more unhappiness than Rose." But I love him.

Eileen's time finally came. On January 18, 1937 she wrote in her diary:

> We fixed up Box Car Bertha again to our delight. . . . Hy Simons, 20 year newspaper friend . . . was in—Ben read last chapter and he said "Don't let anyone touch the style." I

knew. Ben said he ought to spank me when I cried because I was so tired. I let the manuscript fall. It seemed like my precious baby.

The manuscript was edited one more time by an editor chosen by the publisher. The process went quickly this time and the book was finally published several months later.

Eileen's confidence in Ben has been justified by time. *Sister of the Road:The Autobiography of Box-Car Bertha* as told to Dr. Ben L. Reitman was reprinted at least twice in Ben's lifetime. In the early 1970s, the film *Boxcar Bertha* was released. Produced by Roger Corman, directed by Martin Scorsese, and starring Barbara Hershey as Bertha and David Caradine as her companion, it can still be seen occasionally on late-night cable television. *Sister of the Road* was reprinted by Amok Press in 1988 as *Boxcar Bertha* and was chosen as a Quality Paperback Book Club selection in 1990.

I have no way of knowing whether I was upstaged by the heroine when *Sister of the Road* was finally published, but I do not doubt seeing her in print made my father very happy. After losing the manuscript to Marjorie Peters for almost two years, my father had written to the publisher upon the return of the last section:

> That is the "Gift of the Gods"—to have something grow within you—a poem, a book, a child. . . .

> Half a million men in jails were holding out their hands to me this morning as I trudged through the Park. My back was weighed down by cares. I looked at the sky with its black and blue clouds, behind which the red sun was faintly visible. I thought about "the things that was and is." In fancy May, Emma, Anna, Rose, Eileen and Mecca's mother walked with me and we talked about Mecca, the coming child. . . .

And out of the land of prayers and desires there came a beautiful, strong, passionate woman. She put her arms around me and all else was forgotten. My soul was seduced. It was Box Car Bertha. She had just gotten out of jail and was as lovely and virile as ever. When I looked at her I said, "Box Car Bertha, take me. These other women were my sweethearts and the men my friends, but you are my heart."

SIXTEEN

Soap and Water

We must make sex safe, foolproof.
—*Ben Reitman in "VDC Report 96," 1938*

In 1927 my father was at the height of his professional career as a venereal disease specialist. His income reflected the prosperity of his underworld patients, and he had invitations to speak at bohemian clubs and universities all over Chicago. In short, when he was as "successful" as he would ever be, he went to see Emma in Canada. After attending one of her lectures, he wrote her a harshly critical letter complaining that "the old mommy is no more. The great giant of the platform was not in Essex Hall."

Emma, exiled from her chosen country, depressed and uncertain how she would find the money needed to start her autobiography, responded with fire:

> It is you who are dead, not I. I may not have been as great as when we both went from success to success, but I am as a matter of fact more alive than ever. For I have learned through tears and blood that the intrinsic human value is not successful meetings, or the adulation of the public, or much publicity. The only enduring and abiding value is the capacity to stand out against friend and foe, to be inseparably allied with the future. Can you say that of yourself?

I do not know what my father replied to Emma's question,

but for me, Ben's answer is an unqualified yes. Although the causes he shared with Emma were largely behind him by 1927, his lifetime efforts to educate and improve the health of hoboes addressed conditions of the homeless that are with us today.

But Ben's single most important crusade alone was still to come. Unlike his contemporaries in the local and national medical establishment, my father recognized early in the 1920s that prevention was the key to controlling venereal disease. He would be most closely "allied to the future" during the Chicago Syphilis Control Program of 1937-1938 when his outspoken and unpopular efforts on behalf of venereal disease prevention would foreshadow national public health policy more than fifty years later. It would take the AIDS crisis to make national public policy address many of the ideas my father had championed.

In December 1936 Surgeon General Thomas Parran, Jr., who had been making national headlines with his frank approach to the previously taboo subject of syphilis, called a National Conference on Venereal Disease Control. Syphilis and gonorrhea were serious public health problems, he explained. It was estimated that one in ten Americans had syphilis. Compounding the problem during the Depression were the cost of medical treatment and the length of time it took one to become cured—usually from one to three years. Unable to afford private treatments or find public clinics, many persons infected with syphilis did not seek treatment or, if they did, would not complete treatments once diagnosed. As with early AIDS patients, persons with syphilis also had difficulty finding doctors to treat them and hospitals to admit them. Gonorrhea, although not potentially fatal like syphilis, was another serious problem with over 700,000 new cases reported annually.

Shortly before Chicago Board of Health Commissioner Herman Bundesen and his administrators left for the Surgeon

General's conference, Ben wrote them a letter. While acknowledging that "Chicago has the largest and best Venereal Disease Clinics in America, and probably in the world," he pointed out there were still problems in the city that needed attention. He recommended the department establish new clinics in areas of highest risk: the black district on Chicago's South Side where twenty percent of the population was estimated to have venereal disease; the West Side hobo district where fifteen percent of the population was infected; and the North Side "Hobohemia" district with the "very active and multiple sex life" of its prostitutes, pimps, homosexuals, drug addicts and criminals. Nonresidents "slumming" at the cabarets and dives in the area were also at high risk, he emphasized.

Ben concluded his letter:

> Gentlemen, I realize you are human, and that you have pride and prejudice and a sense of ownership of diseases in Chicago, and you hesitate to share the glory of ridding Chicago of diseases with any one. I beg of you to put your individual ambitions aside and think in terms of Chicago with less venereal and infectious disease. I am looking for a job. I can help you.

Ben had been negotiating with the Board of Health for a position in venereal disease control since the Venereal Disease Division had been reorganized the previous spring. Probably no other physician in Chicago knew its high-risk populations as well as he or felt as comfortable with them. These assets were offset by the probability that no other physician in Chicago had Ben's reputation for generating backlash when it came to controversial subjects.

When Mayor Kelly called a meeting of Chicago's venereal disease experts in January 1937, Ben was invited to give his views. He declined after a warning from Commissioner Bundesen reminded him how badly he wanted a job. Ben and

Bundesen reached a compromise when Ben started the Chicago Society for the Prevention of Venereal Disease, an organization that consisted of himself as director, and Eileen and a few others as volunteer secretaries. He could now correspond or speak freely about prevention in the name of the society, without implicating the Chicago Board of Health.

Following the December 1936 conference in Washington, Surgeon General Parran moved quickly to liberalize federal policy towards venereal disease. With the backing of President Roosevelt, and surprisingly strong public support, Parran began pumping federal monies into city and state health departments around the country for diagnostic examinations for syphilis and the distribution of antisyphilitic drugs.

Despite his determination not to sound moralistic, Parran had strong reservations about emphasizing prevention of venereal disease because of the implication that preventive measures encouraged sexual behavior. Detection and treatment became the cornerstones of Parran's national campaign.

In early 1937 the Chicago Syphilis Control Program was initiated under the leadership of Commissioner Bundesen. Ben was hired as a special investigator on the federal payroll, but attached to the Chicago Board of Health. He was assigned to investigate and report on the origins of, and possible solutions to, the syphilis and gonorrhea problems in the same black, skid-row, and red-light districts he had so aptly described in his earlier letter.

In addition to his specific assignment, Ben felt free to write reports on federal and local venereal disease statistics, as well as on relevant books and articles his superiors might not have seen. He also included his views on the wisdom and error of the Health Department's ways in dealing with venereal disease control and other social and health problems in Chicago. For variety, he included colorful vignettes of his clientele and updates on his correspondence and activities as director of the Chicago Society for the Prevention of Venereal Disease. During his employment Ben wrote 300 reports which offer a unique insight into public health in Chicago during the last of the Depression years. Ben also took officials on tours, pleading for better understanding of the high-risk populations they were serving.

Shortly after he was hired, Ben took up the cause for venereal disease prevention in an article and interview that was published in the University of Chicago magazine, *Phoenix*:

> Can you catch syphilis by kissing or from towels? Yes, about as easy as you can come through four years of study in one year with straight "A"s. In the last fifteen years, I've had 5,000 patients in my office. I've worked in the Social Hygiene League, the Jail Clinic and the Municipal Venereal Disease Clinic, and am familiar with the clinics of Detroit, New York, London, and Paris, and I never saw a half dozen cases of syphilis in my life that were not the result of sexual contact.

This was hardly the official line of the medical and public health establishment in 1938. A pamphlet, *Help Stamp Out Syphilis*, jointly published by the Chicago Medical Society and the Chicago Health Department, advised, "Syphilis is a venereal disease which is highly infectious. . . . In most cases the disease is spread from one person to another by sexual contact, although a person may be innocently infected. . . . The disease may be contacted by kissing, using drinking cups, towels and personal articles." It would be another fifty years before Surgeon General C. Everett Koop delivered his unprecedented message about AIDS to every American household: "You can become infected by having sex—oral, anal or vaginal—with someone who has the AIDS virus. . . . You won't get AIDS from a kiss. . . . You won't get AIDS from clothes, a telephone or a toilet seat."

From the beginning of the Chicago Syphilis Control Program, Ben emphasized prevention in his reports, articles, public lectures, and correspondence with public health officials. In a typical statement he wrote:

> The procedure for prevention is unbelievably simple. Rubber preventatives [condoms] are fairly reliable when intelligently used by a sober person. And just as a man can put his finger in typhoid or tuberculosis germs and wash them off without ever [getting] any infection, so soap and water and immediate voiding after contact gives protection.

During the early 1920s, Commissioner Bundesen shared Ben's views and daringly suggested that Chicago's vice lords include the cost of a prophylactic kit containing condoms and powders for douching or washing in the price of the prostitute's services. The women were also to be encouraged to instruct their male patrons in the use of condoms. However, his early slogan, "If you can't be moral, you must be clean," provoked a storm of newspaper, public and medical protest. Always politically astute, Bundesen reversed his position. The emphasis on prevention was replaced by an emphasis on detection and treatment of infected persons, and quarantine of uncooperative houses of prostitution.

At the time Ben was hired, his supervisors were sympathetic to his efforts, but cautious that public opinion might view an emphasis on prevention by the Health Department as encouraging immoral behavior. "We're going to do it, but we've got to be careful," Louis Schmidt, Ben's supervisor, told him. "I don't want you to go to the YWCA and shock the women, but if you go to the hoboes and the underworld and to certain groups, and use good judgement, you can go ahead and talk about prophylaxis and prevention."

Within two months on the job, Ben also met directly with Surgeon General Parran and showed him what he called a "family prophylactic package" which was similar to the kit recommended by the Chicago Health Department in Bundesen's more liberal days. Ben suggested that giving these packages away to infected persons in public clinics or selling them to private patients would be a cheap and positive approach to the problem. There is no record of my father's conversation with the surgeon general, but it's likely that he told Parran what he often said in his reports: "You can't teach people with syphilis and gonorrhea to abstain from sex any more than you can teach well people to abstain."

Unfortunately, this was not the view held by the surgeon general. Parran, a devout Catholic, preferred what he called "moral prophylaxis" or abstinence outside of marriage. In 1937 he wrote, "It is the utmost importance for us in the United States to encourage the education of our young people to decent living through all the means at our command of church, school, official and voluntary agency."

Diametrically opposed to Parran's concept of sex education for the young, my father believed in answering the questions that young people asked:

"How can you tell if a girl is hot?"

"How many times can a boy masturbate without hurting himself?"

"How long does it take to tell if you've caught something or not?"

"How do girls jack off?"

These were sample questions from one of his youthful audiences which he presumably answered.

My father also argued that since young women were just as willing to indulge in sexual activity as boys, it was wrong to protect girls from realistic sex education in schools. "We believe a time will come when condoms will be on exhibition in high schools," he boldly predicted.

Parran may not have expressed his reservations initially to Ben or, more likely, Ben may not have listened to any subtle objections to his views. In either case, hoping for additional publicity for his prophylactic package, Ben described his interview with the surgeon general to a *Washington Post* reporter: "Clinics and treatments will never solve any problem for that is the work at the sewer end."

After a few months on the job, Ben wrote his friend William Evans:

> Everyone agrees that prophylaxis is essential to a venereal disease campaign, but they tell me to hold my horses. . . . I am trying so hard to work in harmony with my bosses but you know my tendency to step out of line, run ahead, and wave the red flag. I am so grateful to have my job and earn $150 a month, support my family and pay my debts.

As much as he loved his work, my father's reports also reflect his awareness of its relative insignificance within the greater context of the Depression. On Thanksgiving, he attended Mother Greenstein's free dinner for the homeless with Eileen. There, he concluded:

> Our talk on syphilis control and prevention was decidedly out of place. These men wanted food, a cigar, a drink. Lovingly we gave it to them, and for the half an hour they sat at the table with us they smiled and joked. But when they left, they went out to darkness, homelessness. . . . The incidence of syphilis and gonorrhea was high [among the homosexuals and women], but there are conditions worse than venereal disease—poverty, unemployment, a bleak future. The brains of the world is now concentrated on syphilis. Let's get rid of syphilis so that we can take up the problem of poverty.

In a report titled, "I Was Walking Down Northpark Doing No Harm/and Along Comes A Whore and She Grabs Me By the Arm," Ben reported that a black prostitute told him,

"There's more colored people that die than are born in one year? Well, you tell them for me that we need jobs more than we need blood tests."

By early 1938 the passage of the federal Venereal Disease Control Act provided massive federal funding for new programs. Because of the success of its earlier efforts, Chicago was chosen to become a model city for Parran's new federal directives. A questionnaire sent to one million Chicago residents asked if they would be willing to take an anonymous blood test for syphilis. The overwhelmingly positive response convinced officials, and testing stations were established throughout the city in public clinics, public buildings, and city parks. At the height of the program, 10,000 to 12,000 individuals per day were tested in what Parran called "the Wasserman dragnet."

With the start-up of the testing program, Ben was assigned to solicit for blood testing in places as diverse as flophouses and public parks in middle class neighborhoods. Given his lively and enthusiastic manner, he was uniquely suited for the job as a "roper." When he was later commended to Bundesen for his effectiveness by Lawrence Linck, the director of the Syphilis Control Program, Ben reviewed his history in his response:

> The Syphilis Control Program seems so easy and respectable. . . . Birth control and antiwar propaganda, the IWW and the anarchist propaganda meant jail, tar and feathers, ostracism. So now when we stand in front of a dragnet station and have people respond to our entreaty and thank us for inviting them in, it's easy and such a joy.

> And yet, we are not altogether happy. . . . It's very painful to realize that some of the fine young men and women who have taken a blood test at our solicitation will someday become infected with gonorrhea and syphilis, especially

when we feel a word of warning, a leaflet, would save them.

Foreshadowing today's public health measures, my father was convinced that clients needed to be reached where they lived, and be spoken to in a language they could clearly understand. In his capacity as director of the Chicago Society for the Prevention of Venereal Disease, he spoke in churches, clubs, outdoor forums, and high schools. He also spoke in patrol wagons full of prisoners, and in houses of prostitution, pool rooms, flophouses, and taverns. Ben also made a special effort to teach prophylaxis to the "sexateers": men who lectured on sex in bohemian clubs, showed sexually explicit movies, or sold sex manuals and magazines. Who would need the information better than their customers?

His vocabulary drew a reprimand from his supervisor Schmidt, who warned him "not to be so vulgar and sexy and to talk so plainly." Throwing oil on the fire, Ben added in his next report, "Unto the lewd, all things are lewd."

By late in the Depression, much of Chicago's population was reduced to making a living wherever possible. Sex was cheap, but at least it was still selling. Ben observed:

If the town is tight or closed up, there's no evidence of it. Prostitutes can be seen in large numbers in all parts of town. Street walkers, both black and white, are more common in Chicago than for a long time. Window tapping can be heard on both the West and South sides. Street walkers are common and brazen. The whores are verbose. Invite them to have a drink and they'll talk about their work. Homosexuals ply their trade on the North, West and South sides in the open. Sex—sex—everywhere.

My father was not above supplementing his own income by conducting tours of these areas for "respectable people." A tour for students arranged by the YMCA and "a group of Gary women" who wanted to visit "some of the Bohemian places and also some really slummy places" were typical examples.

By May 1938 Ben was growing increasingly impatient. Despite increased funding for detection and treatment, funds for prevention were still woefully inadequate. Ben was also painfully aware that grossly misleading articles, ads in the newspapers, and the scare tactics used by the Health Department were only thinly veiled attempts to warn people against sexual activity. When the newspapers reported increased federal raids on drugstores selling condoms, he wrote bitterly, "When people become enlightened and no longer fear diseases as punishment the moralists have lost their influence. . . . The historians are following every phase of the syphilis drive."

Whether or not the surgeon general developed a personal vendetta against my father—as some of Ben's friends suggested to him—increased pressure from Parran on the Chicago Health Department to de-emphasize prophylaxis made the termination of Ben's employment inevitable. At the Industrial Safety Congress held in October 1938 in Chicago, Ben publicly asked Dr. A. E. Russell, who was speaking on the role of industry in the control of venereal disease, to say a few words about prophylaxis. Russell replied, "I'm sorry I can't do it. Headquarters [United States Public Health Service] does not look upon venereal prophylaxis favorably." When Ben asked why, Russell gave Parran's standard reply: "The clergy, the women's clubs, and the decent people are opposed to it."

During the question-and-answer period, Ben identified himself as representing the Chicago Society for the Prevention of Venereal disease and made the following speech:

> What would you say if we told you that the machinery shops in a big industry were killing and maiming thousands and then said, "We have a splendid hospital and fine surgeons to take care of the dying and wounded. Syphilis is a

preventable disease. No one ever need catch it. Wash the parts with soap and water and etc. Put a placard up in all of your industries. "It pays to be decent. Be loyal to your wife. Extramarital contacts are dangerous. If you indulge, use prophylactics."

When he returned to the office that afternoon, he was fired by his supervisor. Pressed for an explanation, my father later wrote Lawrence Linck, "Schmidt was genial but Bundesen was furious." Philosophically sympathetic to the idea of prophylaxis and respectful of Ben's largely solitary efforts with high-risk populations, Bundesen had given him enormous latitude in his activities with the Health Department. Inexcusably to Bundesen, Ben had bitten the hand that fed him by confronting Russell at the Safety Congress.

My mother was then also working for the Chicago Health Department as a bacteriologist, although under the name of Oliver. Ironically, the official reason given my father for being fired was, "there are two members of your family on the payroll." He added in his letter to Linck, "There are several valid reasons for discharging me but no one mentioned any of them."

SEVENTEEN

I Pass on Life
to My Children

Through my children I shall roll down through the ages
    and become immortal. . . .
I am so proud and humble to be a Father. I will fear
    no evil.
I have wanted and worked for a better world for all
    children.
And I have loved life, all of it.

                —Ben Reitman to friends, 1940

By the time my father was fired from the Chicago Syphilis Control Program, my father and mother had been living together for almost two years. It was a difficult time for my mother. Whatever fragile reconciliation she had achieved with my grandparents by the first year after my birth was threatened by Rose's surprise visit to Houston in December 1937. Although Rose had not seen Ben for several years, a letter from either Ben or a Chicago friend about his activities must have triggered her fury.

According to Ben's version of the story, Rose denounced him to my grandfather as a "liar, thief, betrayer of young girls, an anarchist, and a crook out to get their money." She also claimed Ben had driven May Reitman and Sarah Watchmaker insane, and had killed Brutus's mother Anna. "You can imagine all the things Rose told him, mostly true," Ben commented to his friend Theodore Schroeder. Rose concluded her tirade by offering to divorce Ben to allow him to marry Medina if the Olivers would replace the money he had stolen from her.

As hurt as my grandparents had been by what they considered my mother's immoral behavior, the prospects of being blackmailed by Rose and having Ben as a son-in-law were even worse. The version of the story my mother told me more than fifteen years later was that Rose had asked my grandfather Oliver for $5,000 for "heart balm," and he had refused to give it to her. She did not elaborate on why Rose thought she deserved it, and as many times as I heard the story, I never asked.

At the time of the event, my mother was equally laconic in a letter to Brutus, away vacationing with a college friend. She ended her letter with a one-line summary: "Rose visited Grandpa Oliver in Texas with grievances and threats because somebody stold her property." This sentence is typical of my mother in that it is open to several interpretations. Certainly Rose thought that my mother had stolen Ben from her.

Although my father would never see my grandparents again, he continued to send them monthly letters in my voice relating family happenings, and insisting that it was they, and not Medina, who were in the wrong. Immediately after Rose's visit, he described my mother to my grandparents: "Mother looks just what she is, 'A beautiful, young happy mother, with security—spiritual security. The kind that love and the consciousness of having done what she wanted to brings.'"

Regardless of my father's assurances of my mother's happiness to her parents, it could not have been easy for her in Chicago. Brutus was living at home while he finished college and was loving and accepting. But Ida Reitman was another matter. Although my grandmother sometimes stayed with other relatives or in rented rooms in the neighborhood, when she was home she treated Medina as she had all of Ben's earlier women. Despite my mother's increasingly larger role in supporting the family as time went on, she later recalled to me that when Ida was angry, the older woman would hiss at her, "When you came here, you didn't have a pot to piss in."

My grandmother's hostility and my mother's silent, but visible response were my earliest lessons in wanting not to know too much. Without anyone telling me directly, I learned there were secrets in our family that I shouldn't know and questions about my father and mother that I shouldn't ask because they hurt my mother.

One of my father's letters described an occasion when my grandmother Reitman encouraged me, at age three or four, to tell my mother that her name was Medina Oliver not Medina Reitman. I can imagine myself as a child watching my mother's sad face in response to what I unknowingly said. My father wrote to my half-sister Jan, "Brave Medina, who stands by me and cannot be frightened or bribed is truly my mate. You women, you paid so dearly for my development."

In the fall of 1938, my grandfather Oliver became seriously ill. It may have been this illness, my father's letters drawing my grandparents back to my mother and me, or some combination that caused my grandparents to invite my mother to Houston during her vacation—her first visit since I had been born two years earlier.

Although Ben assured the Olivers in his next letter from "Mecca," "I doubt if ever Mother was more anxious to see her Father and Mother/ not in all the years she's been away," he added relentlessly, "You never realized what you did to Mother in the days when I first arrived." Medina's description, however, of the warm welcome she and I received suggests that any lack of forgiveness was not shown openly. Ben was the one whom my grandmother Oliver would not forgive. Besides his other failings, his continual raking up of the past would not allow them to forget Medina's status.

My parents' mutual uncertainty about their future together is shown in their exchange of letters during this separation. When Ben suggested that he might leave Chicago for a year to work on a book, Medina replied, "It is a surprise to us that you will be able to do without us for a year, for we do not think we could be away from you that long. However, life is full of surprises."

But Medina's letter is equally revealing in what it doesn't say. There is no mention of Ben's firing from the Health Department the week before Medina left for Houston, or any reassurances that his future would be brighter. Medina may have considered Ben's employment a problem only he could solve. She also may have wondered how she could support Ben, in those Depression years, but the problem was too overwhelming to address directly.

Ben thought there was a good possibility that Medina would not return from Texas. He wrote her:

> I wake up so often in the night and think of you and see you.
> Often you come to me in all of your loveliness, tenderness and sweetness.
> Then some time I see you with a hard Texas face "I don't give a damn what you do." . . .
>
> I am glad I have Mecca, I am grateful for the joy of being her Father. . . .
> And more than anything else your absence, your uncertainty is driving me into a
> Strong desire to write, to do some Religious, Sociological work among the outcasts
> If ever you or Mecca leave me, it is going to take a great deal of work, service and prayer.

My mother did return from Texas, and her paycheck provided our family's income while my father was unemployed. Although Ben wrote numerous letters to his friends and former colleagues asking for a job in public health, he refused to soften his stand on the importance of venereal disease prevention. In turn, Ben's friends were personally supportive but stopped short of agreeing with his position. Nels Anderson, now an administrator in Washington with the W.P.A., wrote to Ben:

> You have been one of my most useful teachers. What I learned from you was a degree of tolerance and understanding of people that was not taught by precept or example in any of the classes I took. . . . What you need is a good course in public administration. I am afraid if you took such a course and it soaked in that the result would be disastrous. Your best friends would no longer recognize you.

In addition to applying for jobs, Ben also explored other sources of income. He inquired of his publisher for *Sister of the Road* whether he would be interested in his 330 reports from the Chicago Syphilis Control Program for a potential book, "or two or three," but the publisher was not encouraging. Ben's later efforts to use his manuscripts and letters for "a history of unemployment and hobo movements" were also not successful. Always hopeful that things would get better, Ben did not stand idle. He continued to see friends and patients in his office, and to speak and correspond on a variety of medical and social issues, keeping his volunteer stenographers busy for four hours a day.

My father's letters to my dying grandfather Oliver are painful to read now. In retelling the story of my birth to my grandparents on my second birthday, he portrayed my mother to her parents as weaker and more helpless than ever. "Poor dear Mother was so timid and frightened, like a dog who had her puppies under the house," he wrote in my voice. When my grandfather was hospitalized, my father wrote heartlessly, "People who have confidence in the cosmos and faith in justice and the future never have to get sick to attract sympathy."

In late January, my grandmother notified my mother that

my grandfather was failing rapidly, and my mother and I left immediately for Houston. My father's letter to my mother in Houston captures her silent pain:

> Yes Dear Medina, Dad is not the only one in your family that needs to get well.
> You need more peace and health vibrations, your coughing is like the
> Rat a tat tat of the Spanish machine guns, something suppressed within you
> Crying out for expression, crying out for change, your lips are silent
> But your lungs and heart rebel.
> Poor dear Medina, Can't take her baby to Sunday School, can't go here or there
> Your courage is wonderful, but the load laid on you by the Tribune God
> Was too much for Father, Mother and You. . . .
> I beg you not to let
> Tradition, man made morality, Mother Grundy [social pressure] ruin your family health and happiness.

My grandfather died shortly after my mother's arrival. Distraught over my grandfather's death, my grandmother accused my mother of killing him with her behavior. As an added blow, she told my mother that her father had changed his will shortly before his death. My mother assumed her share of her father's estate would be given to the University of Texas because of her illegitimate child.

In reading my grandfather's will today, I agree there was a punitive element, but not at the level my mother inferred. The will stated that if my grandmother were also to die, my mother's money would be put in a trust to be managed by her brother. But the overriding consideration for the change was practicality. In the new will, my grandfather left what was formerly his children's half of the estate to my grandmother, thinking she would need income for the rest of her life. My mother had no way of knowing that my generous grandmother would continue to help us for the next thirty years.

In the fall of 1938, through his brother Lew's political connections, Ben was assigned to a temporary position with the Chicago Board of Health doing smallpox vaccinations in hobo shelters. Once again, he wrote reports detailing ways the Health Department could improve its services to hoboes and described the "vicissitudes of a vaccinator." But this time he made a special effort to be careful in public. "Frequently we see newspaper men but never give interviews," he wrote. "We are well aware we must not talk for the Board of Health or the administration and discreetly keep in the background." Unfortunately, discretion did not help; the job lasted only until the next election.

Ben felt increasingly separated from his former activities. At the hobo convention he attended in the spring of 1939, he noted that the hoboes were no longer advocating "direct action and sabotage, confiscating the goods in warehouses, taking over the mines, the factories, the railroads. Now the trend of the hoboes and the communists is to ask the government to do things." Many of his radical friends from his days with Emma had "sunk into oblivion, melancholy and suicide," or were on the relief rolls.

After his last firing, Ben was determined to speak freely, no matter what the consequences. After attending four of his incendiary lectures in Washington Park in one week, Medina told him, "Don't expect me to visit you in jail." Ben commented to Brutus, "Jail, death, infamy, loneliness and even ridicule are preferable to inertia and acquiescence."

My father's preference for ridicule rather than inertia, and his strong need to be remembered, led him to encourage Elmer Gertz and Bruce Milton to proceed with his biography,

"The Clown of Glory: Ben Reitman's Tale." Scheduled for publication in the fall of 1939, the manuscript was far from a flattering portrait, describing both real and fictional details from his sexual adventures as a young hobo through his professional decline. Ben wrote in his introduction to the biography, "To me the book is largely fiction, but for those who choose to believe it, everything in the book is true, only it is worse."

Brutus, concerned about his father's professional future, appealed to Gertz not to publish the book. An even more powerful objection, however, came from another quarter. Emma's friend Fitzi, afraid that unfavorable publicity for Emma would seriously jeopardize her possible return to the United States, asked Ben to hold up publication. Although Ben dismissed Fitzi's objections in his reply to her, his subsequent letter to the authors and publisher documented Fitzi's and Brutus's concerns. Ben believed that Emma was the reason the book was never published.

Despite the efforts of Fitzi and many others, Emma was denied admission to the United States and instead went to Canada in the spring of 1939. After three years of not answering Ben's letters, she reopened correspondence with Fitzi's encouragement. Still critical, she would find some measure of reconciliation with him in her last year of life. Her intense involvement with the Spanish Civil War was behind her, but she was still mourning her loss of Alexander Berkman. Emma found Ben a connection to the most satisfying period of her past.

Warmed by the international tributes she received from her comrades for her seventieth birthday in June, Emma was affirming in her next letter:

> For a man who swears by Jesus you are of faint heart to doubt my feeling about the ten years we spent together. I admit they were for the most part very painful years for me,

and no doubt also for you. But I would not have missed knowing such an exotic and primitive creature as you. . . . You were, in fact, the only man of all the men I had known who completely dedicated himself to the work and aims that were the strongest raison d'etre in my life. . . . You gave me the best, alas, also the worst in you during our ten years.

Emma invited Ben to see her in Canada, but the two were never able meet again.

Ben's untreated diabetes left him feeling ill for much of 1939. Money was difficult to come by, but he did have some income from his medical practice. "Sometimes I think I am better and sometimes worse. Don't be surprised if Mecca becomes your charge someday," he wrote Brutus. Ben added about one of his patients, "Betty's poor judgement in choosing a sweetheart made it possible for me to give the landlord $5 and send you the enclosed $2."

In October, Ben was hospitalized following a stroke and chest pains. Brutus found a construction job to help support the family, and Ben used his illness as an opportunity to panhandle his friends, largely unsuccessfully, from his hospital bed.

Emma responded to one of these letters with a mixture of belittlement of his work and a sympathetic effort to focus his attention on the family she herself did not have:

I felt all along since I have known you that you are entirely too optimistic about the effect of your work and the so-called appreciation, applause and flattery you received. I was afraid that you might wake up some day and find everything so superficial. However, I know you will regain your old happy-go-lucky spirit. . . . I rather think that with your disappointments you have reason to be exceedingly glad. According to your own account, you have a great son, a lovely girl-child, a companion and a lot more. So you are rich, my dear, much more so than tens of thousands of people who have nobody and are wanted nowheres. I am glad that you are not among them.

By December 1939 Ben was able to reopen his office. He wrote to William Evans:

The practice of medicine is humiliating, if not heartbreaking. I do not feel that I have sufficient talent or information to earn an honest living practicing medicine. This business of treating old neurosyphilis and chronic gonorrhea, which is apparently unbenefited by treatment, affords me very little pleasure, although the patients appear willing to pay for it. . . . Please don't get mad or weep. I have no complaints or special needs. I just pass the news on to you.

It amazes me that, in the midst of all of this uncertainty about our family's finances and my father's health, my mother was happy that she had finally become pregnant again. Determined to have the family that she wanted, she again predicted twins. Her hopes were not realized, but my new sister was called "Twinzie" for years.

My mother was not the only woman who was happy with my father. Eileen and Ben saw each other daily. I am sure they continued to be lovers as opportunity and Ben's health permitted. Ben described Eileen to my sister Jan, "She has been my secretary and intimate Comrade and has given me a beautiful devotion and love. I hope you will get acquainted with her."

Ben announced the birth of Medina Benn Reitman in May 1940, thirty-eight years after the birth of Jan, the daughter he had so willingly abandoned. "I hope you will rejoice with us in welcoming our new beautiful little daughter born May 1st," he wrote his friends. "She was no accident, but a child of desire and passion, born into a home of love and unity." He ended the letter, "I pass on life to my children, feeling sure they will get much out of living and service, and hoping they will give more to the better world than I was able to give."

Ben's sensitivity to his own mortality was heightened by his knowledge of Emma's condition. A stroke had left her speechless and paralyzed. Emma died in May 1940 in Toronto. Twenty years after her deportation, the doors of the United States were now open to her. She was buried in Waldheim Cemetery, near the monument to the Haymarket martyrs. Although Ben was interviewed by the Chicago papers, the local anarchists made a point of not asking him to speak at Emma's funeral. He attended anyway, bringing me to the service. He introduced me to a friend afterwards, "This is my little Emma Goldman."

My mother's plans to return to work shortly after my sister Medina was born did not materialize. Ben wrote to a friend, "She was so sorry to lose her job at the City Health Department. Bundesen fired her for having a baby." Ben did not comment whether Commissioner Bundesen thought new mothers should stay home with their babies, or that a second child out of wedlock was even more unacceptable than the first. During her enforced unemployment, my mother took my sister and me for a visit to Texas.

Bundesen's attitude may have been ambiguous, but my grandmother Oliver was clear where she stood. After a week with her family, Medina sent Ben fifty dollars for his railroad fare and asked him to meet her in Texas. "Life is a series of choices," she wrote Ben. "I may not be able to raise the dead; I may not be able to raise money, but it burns me up to be told I won't be able to raise so many children." Unrepentant, she ended another letter, "We love you very much and hope we may make some more babies."

Ben's letters to Houston were supportive and sympathetic. He wrote, "As long as life lasts I will always be with you. . . .

Medina, My Lover, You are a great soul, strong and brave, your children shall rise up and call you blessed. I hope they won't curse me." In a more humorous mood, he added in another letter, "I hope they [your family] ain't worried about having to support me. I will probably be able to make a living until the end. Please let them know that I appreciate being able to get into their corral even if I did have to jump the fence."

The birth of Ben and Medina's second daughter again raised Rose's hopes for a financial settlement. After not having seen Ben for five years, Rose came to Chicago and offered to divorce him. Ben reported that he told her, "I have two lovely babies, I want to keep them. I don't want to have anything to do with you. If you care to stamp my babies bastards, I shall not object." Rose left for California, but corresponded about divorce through the summer.

Reading my father's letters to Rose that summer forces me to a painful conclusion. For all my father's talk about "his babies" and my mother's bravery, his remarks hit the target too unerringly not to be deliberate.

Sure to infuriate Rose by referring to his multiple infidelities, Ben mentions Eileen in his letter as "My Glorious Irish Queen who knows what love and devotion really is and who made it easy for me to respect Christian women." This obvious attempt to disrupt negotiations is only one more piece of evidence that he had no serious intention of ever divorcing Rose, despite his apparent efforts.

In the last months of his life, my father would be even more direct about his relationship with Eileen. Reflecting on how he had responded to "the most compelling forces in our lives—love, sex, marriage and children," he wrote of the final women in his life:

I loved Medina because it was destiny. She gave me life's

greatest gift—immortality in the form of three beautiful daughters. Medina brought beauty, fulfillment, but not completion in my life. . . .

About ten years ago Eileen O'Connor came into my life . . . I was Emma Goldman's janitor. Eileen has been my super-janitor, secretary, comrade lover and pal. If these last ten years have been worth while as a propagandist—and I think they have—Eileen is responsible.

As much as I believe my father loved my sisters and me and admired my mother, as much as I fantasized for years that he would have married my mother had he been able to, the truth is that he wanted it all. Each woman gave him something the other could not. As long as he was married to Rose, neither my mother nor Eileen could claim him. He wanted to keep things just the way they were.

Family life continued, much as before, after Rose's departure. Fortunately for our growing family, my mother did not stay unemployed long. Her pay was not as good in her new job with the state health laboratory, and it was farther to commute, but with my father's limited income and financial assistance from my grandmother Oliver, the family managed to get by. Ben continued to write my grandmother Oliver monthly letters from one daughter or the other detailing our development and expressing the family's appreciation for her help. Ida Reitman still lived with Ben and Medina periodically—presumably no more harmoniously.

It was Brutus who had undergone the most significant change. A dutiful but indifferent pre-med student, he had finally found his true vocation: flying. That summer he entered a special flight-training program that was part of the growing American defense preparation for the Second World War.

Ben's second stroke in August made him focus even more on his children. He wrote his friend Theodore Schroeder:

Today millions of men are in arms killing one another, more millions are sick and in want but I am most disturbed about Twinzie my six month old girl who is teething and has a cold. Jesus, what a wonderful experience it is to rock your six month old baby in the cold long hours of the morning. It is a greater experience than I had when I was going to San Diego to be tarred and feathered. . . . I was not afraid to die in San Diego when I was on the "spot," but now to croak and leave my babies . . . yes life is a beautiful joke.

By the fall of 1941, my mother had found a better paying job, this time in an experimental five-day treatment unit for syphilis at Cook County Hospital. My father took the opportunity to ask her director for a job for himself. There was no responding offer.

Brutus left home for flight-training school that fall. More than with any of his friends, my father's letters to my half-brother express his vacillating feelings in dealing with his own death and the family he would leave behind:

We took the car away from you, you paid for it.
You paid for the house we live in
And we may have to put the burden of the support of the
    family on you
BUT my father never supported me and I never supported
    Helen
And we all lived through it. So you don't need to worry
    about us. . . .
We all have survival qualities.

But three weeks later he was more uncertain. "My time on earth is limited," he wrote. "What will become of my little babies and what will become of mother?"

Ben was also concerned about Brutus's future. He wrote his son, "I do hope you can live a useful social life and will never have to drop bombs on battleships, villages or troop trains. I had so hoped that you could go into a work that would save lives and help human beings."

Despite his dire predictions, my father was still very much alive in the spring of 1942. He wrote Brutus:

> I've been having a most thrilling experience the last few days trying to die, both times on the breast of a woman. I was able to keep up the dramatic and the heroic until the supposedly last moment but one time the telephone bell and another time the need for an urgent bowel movement brought me back to life. And now I am here to tell the story—that if dying is like the experience I had yesterday, it ain't half bad.

Neither experience was likely to have been shared with my mother, who was a week away from the birth of my new sister, Victoria Regina.

"So now Medina has three little girls, all planned and wanted," Ben announced after Victoria's birth in February 1942. "It is wonderful and precious for a child to have a mother and father that wanted and needed her for the fulfillment of their lives. It is delightful to have grandparents and family that love children and take pride in them." He was more realistic in his letter to Brutus a few days later: "As you would expect, her [Medina's] mother was not very happy or cheerful about the blessed event and as usual when a baby comes wrote an unfriendly letter." Ben's third stroke followed less than two months later.

As he followed public health efforts during the war, my father took pride that the ideas that he had fought for so unsuccessfully with the Health Department were finally receiving recognition in the armed services. He was delighted when the 1942 spring issue of *The Military Surgeon* had an article on soap and water as a prophylactic. The Army was also using a realistic film, *Know for Sure*, on syphilis and gonorrhea as well as a pamphlet on venereal disease prophylaxis.

Brutus finished training and joined the Air Corps Ferry Command. He married Dorothy in June despite my father's warning: "I . . . made the same mistake several times and survived it, and my only sins against the Holy Ghost that I could recall were legal marriages." The fears Ben had expressed earlier to Brutus no longer appear in his letters. Describing his joy with his family, despite his continuing inability to find a job, he concluded a letter to his friend William Evans, "Thanks to a few friends who help carry my load and a comrade who has a good job, I manage to get by."

My mother had negotiated with her former medical school in Galveston about readmission on several earlier occasions, but had never taken the makeup exams she was told she needed. In the fall of 1942, with my father's precarious health a major incentive for earning a better income, she enrolled in an anatomy class to prepare for her examinations. Ben kept my grandmother Oliver posted on Medina's efforts at home, in school, and in her career at the hospital. He wrote, "But all in all, life is delightful. Nothing is hard and the struggle, while not easy, is a great pleasure."

Two weeks later my father had a fatal heart attack at home surrounded by his family. My mother recorded his last day in his Bible with what seems numbed detachment:

Ben Louis Reitman M.D. died November 16 at his home at 6826 S. Bishop St. Chicago Illinois of a coronary thrombosis. He had been complaining of pains around the region of the heart in the afternoon. The attack was acute and Ben passed away at 8:05 p.m. after about a half hour of suffering. He was with his mother, Mrs. Ida Reitman, three little daughters

Mecca, Medina and Victoria Regina and wife Medina Oliver Reitman. . . . Ben lived a full and eventful sixty-three years. One of the things he said at the last was that he had done all of the things in his life he had set out to do. He called on his mother and God in his interval of pain.

My mother had one last challenge for the name of Reitman, but this time it was picked up by the Chicago newspapers. On learning of my father's death, Rose telegraphed the Surrogate Court, "Stop all legal proceedings of will until I, the legal widow, arrive in Chicago as soon as possible. . . . You have my sworn statement Medina Oliver is not his widow. (signed) Rose Siegel Reitman." Rose returned to New York with nothing to show for her efforts.

Once Rose was gone, there was no one who cared what my mother chose to call herself. With the significant exception of her workplace—because Oliver was the name on her nursing license, my mother would later assure my sisters and me—my mother became Medina Oliver Reitman.

My father was buried in Waldheim cemetery not far from the monument to the Haymarket martyrs and Emma. When the stone was later placed on his grave, his epitaph irritated the Chicago anarchists, who threatened to dig up the body of such a traitor to their cause. But for my mother, who bought my father's headstone and wrote the epitaph, it was a personal and not a political statement. Knowing what I know now, I think the inscription reflects her generosity:

"Liberty was his life. Liberty in thought, word and deed."

EIGHTEEN

Living My Father's Life

LIFE has always been wonderful and worth-while. . . .
Nothing has been very difficult, or painful, or hard to
    bear.
Been in jail many times, hungry, broke, in debt, fired
    from jobs, tar-and-feathered, neglected,
But I always enjoyed life, never hated or envied anyone
    and really never suffered.

—*Ben Reitman, 1939*

Having met my father late in life through his letters, it took
me by surprise when I joined the long line of women who had
asked themselves the question, "Can I love such a terrible
man?" I also found myself asking their other question, "Did he
really love me?" Knowing all too well the delusions of my
predecessors, I would still answer yes on both counts.

I have no regrets that the full story of my parents and my
early life waited until I was ready to know it. Considering
the time that has elapsed, I am, truly, lucky Ben Reitman's
daughter. Once I was ready to replace the flat black-and-white
picture of my father (inscribed "with devotion" to my mother)
that I remember from my childhood home with the richly
colored three-dimensional version, it was there—waiting for
me. The carboned message, "I am hoping Mecca will want to
know me," which he had put into a bottle (or, more accu-
rately, a file folder) and thrown in the ocean of time, miracu-
lously came to me.

Just as I have changed with time, it has been fascinating,

too, to watch my father change. He wrote in one letter, "It took three families to let me see the 'light'," and it was true. Indifferent to my older half-sister, Jan, he was a better father to my half-brother Brutus. Anna's death drew him even closer to his son. In failing health his last years of life, my father could be more open with Brutus than with anyone else.

I, too, made a father out of him. By living with me—the child he first thought of only as my mother's—he grew to love me. And by the time my two sisters came along, in the last three years of his life, my father could appreciate us all. Had he known he was leaving behind still another little daughter, despite the burden on my mother, it would have pleased him immensely. He knew the life he loved so intensely was limited for him, but he would pass it on to his children.

Whether my father ever learned to love the adult women in his life as much as he loved his mother is much more debatable. Never sexually faithful to one woman, he was unlikely to be faithful to two. Both my mother and Eileen felt needed and loved by Ben—who is to say which woman had the more vivid imagination in constructing her own love story? I have not read any of my father's later letters to Eileen, but I find his correspondence with my mother very loving and touching, even knowing what I know now, fifty years later. The depth of my mother's love for him, both before and after his death, is what matters to me now. If my mother was not the sole "Mrs. Reitman" in Ben's lifetime, she had the title later and the family that she wanted.

I'm sure my father was also easier to love once he wasn't there to challenge any self-deception. The more I have learned about him, the stronger my feelings have become. Self-serving and generous, hypocritical and deeply insightful, dishonest in person but honest with posterity, destructive yet with immense vitality, a crackpot soapboxer with visions for a better world far ahead of his contemporaries—these are only a few of his many contradictions.

Now I like him much less in some ways, and much more in others, than I did as a child. As I, too, have lived through some of my father's experiences, his optimism, his energy to change things, his resilience in the face of disappointments, his refusal to let others set his goals or define who he was, his joy in life, and his efforts to share his thoughts, both in writing and in person, make him a role model for me now. I have come to love a terrible man who is wonderful, too.

But what I love most about my father is his rich and vivid complexity. Each time I read his letters or articles, I find something newly appalling or amusing or touching or inspiring, always bringing the colorful past back to life for me.

No small part of this richness are the women in his life. In looking for my father in their letters, I found new "mothers" in my family that I care about. I have also come to know and love my own mother as a young woman in a way I would not have thought possible.

For all the pain my father caused these remarkable women, he had something powerful to offer them. "You are better and more developed for knowing me," he wrote my mother. She felt strongly it was true for her and, with the possible exception of Rose, it was true for the others as well. The depth of these women's love for Ben, showing me how to love him despite his many weaknesses, makes me glad my mother chose him for my father.

Three years before I was born my mother wrote my father:

You see, sweet, I love you. . . . I adore hearing from you and I like to write. You suit me well enough that I would want a couple of little girls with your genes to remind me of you. There are times when I want them very badly and then again just to see you would be enough and to kiss you would be wonderful.

Notes

Abbreviations used in the Notes:

Archives and personal collections

BU   The Emma Goldman Collection, Special Collections, Boston University

DR   Personal collection of Dorothy Reitman

IISH   International Institute for Social History, Amsterdam, Emma Goldman Collection

MUL   University of Michigan, Ann Arbor, Labadie Collection

RF   Personal collection of Reitman Family (Mecca Carpenter, Medina Gross, Victoria Kapp and Olive Poliks)

SIUC   The Theodore Schroeder Papers, Special Collections/ Morris Library, Southern Illinois University, Carbondale

UIC   Ben L. Reitman Papers, Special Collections, The University Library, University of Illinois at Chicago

UCB   University of California, Berkeley, Emma Goldman Papers Project

Books and manuscripts

FTM   "Following the Monkey," Ben Reitman's unpublished autobiography in the Ben L. Reitman Papers, UIC

LML   *Living My Life,* Vol I and Vol II, Emma Goldman, New York: Dover, 1970

VDC   Venereal Disease Control Reports, Ben Reitman's unpublished reports in the Ben L. Reitman Papers, UIC

Names of individuals

AM   Anna Martindale
BR   Ben Reitman
EG   Emma Goldman
EO   Eileen O'Connor
MO   Medina Oliver
RR   Rose Reitman

Page
7   "I will be remembered by my carbons...": BR to unknown, n.d., 1936, DR.
7   "He hadn't paid the rent...": DR, personal communication, Mar. 1989.

CHAPTER 3: Ida's Son

9   "My obsession with my mother...": BR to EG, May 30, 1929, IISH.
9-10   "In Chicago she lived among her pots and pans...": LML, 518.
10   "still remembers...": Brutus Reitman to BR, July 1, 1935, DR.
10   "A Man who began life as I did...": FTM, 4.
10   Roger Bruns, personal communication, May, 1987.
10   "I was lucky": BR to Theodore Schroeder, Aug. 1, 1942, SIUC.
11   "occasional husbands": BR to Theodore Schroedoer, Oct. 24, 1942, SIUC.
12   "Better that we freeze...": FTM, 19.
12   "Please lady, I'm lost and hungry...": Ibid., 27.
13   "The homecoming was joyous...": Ibid., 78
13   "I made a speedy recovery...": Ibid., 120.
14   "of all men who have been brutal...": Ibid., 74
14   "a mob of crooks who were working the state fair": BR, "Living With Social Outcasts" unpublished manuscript, 1933, UIC.
15   "no other part of my philosophy...": FTM, 38.
15   "My religious life...": Ibid., 49.

CHAPTER 4: From Medical School to the Hobo College

16   "I had a very difficult time...": Ibid., 137.
16-17   "Ben Reitman has done very fine work...": Ibid., 133.
17   "This is to certify...": Ibid.
17   "a short moony spoony romance...": Ibid., 140.
18   "Mecca is a genuine pure joy...": BR to Jan Gay, Nov. 30, 1938, UIC.

Page

19   "I had a very happy year at school...": FTM, 162.

20   "I'm Ben Reitman.": Ibid., 203.

20   "I am an American by birth...": Ibid., 202.

21   "What an opening Class!": BR, "The Hobo College",
      n.d., DR.

21   "unlawful methods"; "making her believe it to
      be...": George W. Amadon to BR, Mar. 26, 1908, UIC.

21-22 "Grace is thirty-six...": BR to George W. Amadon,
       Sept. 17, 1908, UIC.

CHAPTER 5: My God Emma, How Can You Stand Ben?

23   "The ordinary things that make radicals...": FTM, 213.

24   "more generous to herself...": MO to BR, Dec. 25, 1933,
      DR.

24   "Movements such as the labor movement...": MO,
      n.d., 1946, RF.

24-25 Significant publications about Emma Goldman include
       Candace Falk, *Love, Anarchy, and Emma Goldman*,
       Rutgers University Press, New Brunswick: 1990;
       Alice Wexler, *Emma Goldman: An Intimate Life*,
       New York: Pantheon Books, 1984; Alix Kates Shulman,
       "Living Our Life," in *Between Women* (L. De Salvo,
       S. Ruddick, eds.), Boston: Beacon Press, 1984;
       and Alice Wexler, *Emma Goldman in Exile*, Boston,
       Beacon Press, 1989. The earliest book to identify
       Emma's place in American history is Richard Drinnon,
       Rebel in Paradise, Chicago: University of Chicago Press,
       1961.

26-27 The best description of Ben Reitman's early efforts
       in hobo reform is in Roger Bruns, *The Damndest
       Radical: The Life and World of Ben Reitman, Chicago's
       Celebrated Social Reformer, Hobo King, and Whorehouse
       Physician*, Urbana: University of Illinois Press,
       1987, Ch. 4.

27   "She had a powerful face...": FTM, 216.

27   "My visitor was a tall man...": LML, 415-416.

Page
27 "She had the voice of the angel Gabriel...": FTM, 219.
28 "That night...I was caught in a torrent...": LML, 420.
28 "Flames were shooting from my fingertips": Ibid.,422.
28 "I resolved to have him...": Ibid., 425.
29 "I have another little pamphlet here...": FTM, 243.
29 "we sold more books...": Ibid.
29 "The ordinary listener...": Ibid., 244.
29 "Before Emma Goldman, most of my crimes...": BR to Theodore Schroeder, Aug. 1, 1942, SIUC.
30 "Sister, how old was the baby...": FTM, 235.
30 "Much that I know about the world...": FTM 257 cited in Paul E. Kuhl, ICarbS, Vol. II, No. 1, 1975, 13.
30 "who could love the woman in me...": LML, 433.
30 "the most emphatic chapter in my life...": BR to Theodore Schroeder, Aug. 1, 1942, SIUC.
31 "Voltairine de Cleyre used to say...": BR to Leonard Abbott, June 15, 1940, UIC.
31 "You are too ready to assume...": BR to Hauser and Leonard Abbott, Sept. 16, 1942, UIC.
32 "I sat numb...": LML, 440.
32 "If Emma Goldman could live...": "Ben Reitman's Tale," unpublished manuscript, Bruce Milton and Elmer Gertz, by permission, UIC.
32 "I have propagated freedom in sex": LML, 441.
33 "Please, please write me every day...": EG to BR, July 31, 1911, UIC.
33 "I hold you close.": BR to EG, July 31, 1912, BU and UIC.
34 "One very gentle businessman...": FTM, 283.
35 "Ben lay in a rear car...": LML, 500.
35 "The Times does not commend...": Los Angeles Times, May 19, 1912, cited in Bruns, The Damndest Radical, 124.
35-36 "The cannibals who tarred and feathered...": Eugene Debs, Appeal to Reason, May 25, 1912, cited in Bruns, The Damndest Radical, 124.

CHAPTER 6: I am Always Behind Some Group,
Some Woman

Page
37   "Of course the fact...": FTM, 359.
37   "I left San Diego a beaten man...": Ibid., 285.
37-38 "I understood her very well.": Ibid., 518.
38   "Emma at fifty surpassed any woman...":
      FTM, 361.
38   "I began to realize the wisdom...": LML, 527.
39-40 "Moses Harman": in *Woman's Body, Woman's Right*,
      Linda Gordon, New York: Viking Press, 1976, 217.
40   "Children do not need to be born...": BR,
      Why and How the Poor Should Not Have Children,
      New York: Mother Earth Publishing Association,
      1913, DR.
40   "The time had come...": LML, 553.
40-42 "anti-war topics, the fight for Caplin and Schmidt...":
      Ibid., 555.
41   "his letters breathed a serenity...": Ibid., 573.
41   "You have a child...": Ibid., 581.
41   "they have always given me a fair deal...":
      FTM, 213.
42   "Free-born Americans had to be forcibly pressed...":
      LML, 597.
42   "The young woman of his Sunday class...": Ibid., 613.
42   "tattered and scattered ends...": FTM, 367.
42   "the opponents of the war...": Ibid., 357.
43   "a novelty, a boy, a janitor, a clown...": Ibid., 362.
43   "I feel certain that, had Emma Goldman...":
      Ibid., 359.
43   "In the RED NETWORK...": BR to Jennie, June 29, 1935,
      UIC.
43-44 "I felt the solemnity of the occasion...": FTM, 367.

CHAPTER 7: A Free and Glorious Mother

45   "Business was good.": FTM, 376.
46   "I eat her up.": BR to EO, March 22, 1933, DR.

Page

46-47   Recent publications dealing with Anna Martindale
         include Roger Bruns, *The Damndest Radical*, Chap. 24,
         and Suzanne Poirier, "Emma Goldman, Ben Reitman
         and Reitman's Wives," *Women's Studies*, 1988, Volume 14,
         277-297.

46   "worked like hell for a paltry wage...": Frank Beck,
         Hobohemia, West Ringe, N.H.: Richard R. Smith
         Publisher, 1956, 42.

46-47   "I want no one but you...": BR to EG, July 27, 1912, BU
         and UIC.

47   "I had always thought of Chicago...": FTM 366.

47   "When I was released...": Ibid., 362.

48   "The house was artistically decorated...": Ibid., 369.

48   "From the very first day I opened my office...":
         Ibid., 371.

49   Background on venereal disease is in *No Magic Bullet*,
         expanded edition, Allan M Brandt, New York: Oxford
         University Press, 1987, Chap. 3.

49   "The clinic hours were social hours.": FTM, 374.

50   "Sunday night meetings...": Ibid. 375; background on
         the Dill Pickle is in BR, "Highlights in Dill Pickle
         History", DR.

50   "No matter how rotten...": FTM, 375.

50   "I don't know of anything more glorious...":
         Ibid., 376.

50   "It was strange to see...": Ibid., 368.

50   "breathing the old assurance...": LML, 369.

51   "Whether it was the defeat...": Ibid.

51   "Jail was always a delightful place...": "Prisons in My
         Life", *Phoenix*, 19 (May 1937), 11-24.

51   "To see men suffer and die is terrible...": BR to AM,
         May 11, 1918, DR.

52-53   "Ben" in "The Outcast Narratives", UIC and RF.

53   "The starting of the little life...": AM to BR, n.d., DR.

53-54   "I got a lot of love in jail...": BR to Theodore Schroeder,
         Oct. 24, 1942, SIUC.

54   "disappointed his wife a little...": FTM, 394.

Page

54   "she was lovesick and hypnotized by him": W. Uretz to
      BR, Mar. 3, 1924, RF; BR, "Living With Social Outcasts",
      "Women who go crazy about men", 2-4, UIC.

54   "I read my Bible...": FTM, 394.

55   "treated thousands of men and women...": FTM, 395.

55   "One day I was shooting Salvarsan...": FTM, 396.

56-57 "I was glad to have been in Chicago...": EG to BR,
      Dec. 12, 1919, UIC, cited in Falk, *Love, Anarchy and
      Emma Goldman*, 292-293.

57   "Emma": in "The Outcast Narratives", RF and UIC.

      CHAPTER 8: Her Fragrant Ashes Rest in
                 My Bedroom Now

58   "If you will remember, Evans...": BR to William Evans,
      Oct. 26, 1939, UIC.

58   "I'm ambitious to push up our savings account now.":
      BR to AM, n.d., UIC.

59   "vivid, alive, awake...": *Chicago Herald and Examiner*,
      April 27, 1924, UIC.

59-60 Jan Gay's publications include *On Going Naked*, New
      York: Holborn House, 1932 and four children's books in
      collaboration with Zhenya Gay: *Pancho And His Burrow*,
      New York: William Morrow, 1930; *The Goat That
      Wouldn't Be Good*, New York: William Morrow, 1930;
      The Shire Colt, New York: Doubleday Doran, 1931; and
      The Mutt Book, New York: Harper and Brothers, 1932.

60   "must have eaten into her soul...": Beck, *Hobohemia*, 43.

60   "a decent and proud mother...": Ibid.

60   "periodic gloom and depressions": BR to AM,
      Aug. 27, 1919, UIC.

60   "Anna lived an inner life...": BR to EO, Mar. 28, 1933, DR.

60-61 "You will admit they are very impersonal.": AM to BR,
      n.d., [1919], UIC.

61   "Dear Little Wife": BR to AM, April 22, 1919, UIC.

61   "I believe God as great work...": BR to AM, Oct., 1923,
      UIC.

Page
61-62   "If I were to describe myself...": BR to AM, n.d., UIC.

62   "I see the little Mother...": BR to AM, n.d., UIC.

63   "Venereal Disease—Keep Out": Ben Reitman, *The Second Oldest Profession*: A Study of the Prostitute's "Business Manager", New York: The Vanguard Press, 1931, 97.

63   "much zestful conversation, indiscriminate caresses...": Ben Reitman, "The Joys and Hazards of Sex", Ch. 21, 4, UIC.

63-64   "God's Kingdom for Hobos..."; "all day and all night...": FTM, 422.

64   "The sex urge cannot be controlled...": FTM, 414.

65   The description of prophylaxis used by prostitutes is in Reitman, *The Second Oldest Profession*, 95-110.

65   "We pay for the treatment of any man...": FTM, 416A.

65   Herman Bundesen's role in syphilis prevention and treatment in Chicago is discussed by Suzanne Poirier in *Chicago's War on Syphilis, 1937-1940: The Times, The Trib and the Clap Doctor*, Urbana: University of Illinois Press, 1995.

65   "is positively the most bitter...": BR to AM, April 10, 1926, UIC.

66   "She is gloomy...": BR to AM, April 13, 1926, UIC.

66   "The worst I would do...": BR to EG, Jan 2, 1928, UIC, cited in Falk, *Love, Anarchy, and Emma Goldman*, 373.

67   "becoming instead a caretaker...": Suzanne Poirier, "Emma Goldman, Ben Reitman and Reitman's Wives," *Women's Studies*, 1988, Volume 14, 292.

67   "security, home, haven"; "My weakness, my multiple emotions and needs...": BR to AM, n.d. [1928], UIC.

67   "there should be a legal law ceremony.": BR to AM, n.d., [1928], UIC

67-68   "I wonder if you feel as I do...": AM to BR, n.d., UIC.

68   "The thing that has held us together...": AM to BR, n.d., UIC.

68   "It was inevitable that something like this would happen...": AM to BR, n.d., UIC.

Page
69   "so far different from the usual..."; "currently filling an
       engagement...": Beck, *Hobohemia*, 40.
69   "With one arm Doc enfolds...": Ibid., 45.
69   "I used to weary you...": BR to EG, June 9, 1930, IISH,
       cited in Falk, *Love, Anarchy, and Emma Goldman*, 391.
69-70 "I took her love, her devotion...": BR to MO,
       Jan. 26, 1933, DR.

CHAPTER 9: A Texan at Heart and an Alien
            Everywhere Else

71   "Though she is an honest hard-working loyal mother...":
       BR to Theodore Schroeder, Aug. 26, 1942, SIUC.
72   "wore riding britches to ride hoseback...": Eugene
       Oliver, Jr., personal communication, May, 1986.
72   "I haven't the gift of being very happy...": MO to BR,
       Sept. 1, 1932, DR.
73   "Dr. Keiller called me a fool...": MO, n.d., [1961], RF.
73   "Miss Oliver had considerable difficulty...": Dean of the
       Medical School, Sept. 12, 1930, RF.
73   "she got into a wrangle...": Eugene Oliver Jr., personal
       communication, May, 1986.
74   "I hope you avoid living your life...": Eugene Oliver to
       MO, [January], 1931, RF.
74   "a Texan at heart...": BR to Inez Oliver, Dec. 30, 1939, UIC.
74   "Come when you can, sister...": MO, n.d., 1961, RF.
74-75 "a superb showman...": Beck, *Hobohemia*, 37.
75   "It was quite a chilly day...": MO, n.d., 1961, RF
75   "I have told it so many times..."; his diabetes and
       nephritis...": MO, n.d., 1961, RF.

CHAPTER 10: The Fates Give Us Our Wives

76   "I married Rose...": BR to Theodore Schroeder,
       Aug. 26, 1942, SIUC.
77   "Dearest Mommy": BR to EG, Aug. 23, 1930, IISH, cited
       in Falk, *Love, Anarchy, and Emma Goldman*, 392.

Page

78   "such a weakling as great women...": Harry Kemp,
     Tramping on Life, New York: Boni and Liveright, 1922,
     cited in Falk, *Love, Anarchy, and Emma Goldman*, 392.

78   "Did they all hate Ben...": Agnes Ingles to EG,
     Jan. 6, 1931, MUL, cited in Falk, *Love, Anarchy, and
     Emma Goldman*, 392.

78   "Old Benie dear": EG to BR, 1923, UIC.

78   A detailed analysis of Emma's autobiography is in
     Wexler, *Emma Goldman in Exile*, Boston: Beacon
     Press, 1989, 131-156.

78-79   "that I have nothing left...": EG to Alexander Berkman,
        Feb. 20, 1929, *Nowhere At Home: The Letters from Exile of
        Emma Goldman and Alexander Berkman*, ed. Richard
        Drinnon and Anna Maria Drinnon, New York: Shocken,
        1975, 145, cited in Wexler, *Emma Goldman in Exile*, 138.

79   "We all have something to hide.": EG to Alexander
     Berkman, Dec. 1927, IISH, cited in Falk, *Love, Anarchy,
     and Emma Goldman*, 10.

80   "young, beautiful and playful": BR to Theodore
     Schroeder, August 26, 1942, SIUC.

80   "I dedicate this book...": Reitman, *Second Oldest
     Profession*, dedication.

80   "You are going to write a great autobiography...": BR to
     EG, Dec. [24], 1930, IISH, cited in Falk, *Love, Anarchy,
     and Emma Goldman*, 393.

80   "Ben not only lacks the ability...": EG to Alice Inglis,
     Jan. 26, 1930, MUL, cited in Falk, *Love, Anarchy and
     Emma Goldman*, 395.

80   Information on the reception of *The Second Oldest
     Profession* is from Roger Bruns, personal communication
     and Bruns, *The Damndest Radical*, 260-261.

80   "That Ben is accepted...": EG to Frank Heiner,
     Dec. 24, 1935, IISH.

81   "Dear Cautious Jew Rose": BR to RR, June, 1931, DR.

82   "I thought I could reform him.": Ruth Highberg,
     personal communication, Jan. 1989.

Page

82 "that red rat Retta": BR to EO, April 20, 1933, DR.

82 "I suppose God knows his business.": BR to Nels Anderson, Nov. 18, 1930, UIC.

82-83 "She has a strange hold on me...": BR to "Blue Eyes", July 3, 1936, DR.

83 "an incredible assortment...": Bruns, *The Damndest Radical*, 262.

83 "My dear Mommy": BR to EG, Dec. 6, 1931. IISH, cited in Falk, *Love, Anarchy, and Emma Goldman*, 399-400.

84 "He tells me I have taken...": EG to Agnes Inglis, Dec. 8, 1931, IISH, cited in Falk, *Love, Anarchy, and Emma Goldman*, 399.

84 Emma's failure to "get out of her skin" is portrayed throughout Falk, *Love, Anarchy, and Emma Goldman* and Wexler, *Emma Goldman: An Intimate Portrait* and *Emma Goldman in Exile*.

84 "By no manner of means...": EG to Freemont Older, Dec. 19, 1931, Bancroft Library, University of California, Berkeley, cited in Wexler, *Emma Goldman in Exile*, 149.

84-85 "I want my Ben.": RR to BR, [Dec.] 1932, DR.

85 "Why don't you give your wife a chance?": MO to BR, [Mar. 25, 1932], RF.

85-86 "The truth is you have only your mother—": RR to BR, n.d., [1932], DR.

86 "Yes, Ben, you care for the desolate...": RR to BR, n.d., [1932], DR.

86 "I want you to deal with people...": RR to BR, Sept. 16, 1932, DR.

87 "Your specific charge...": BR to RR, Oct. 22, 1932, DR.

87-88 "I am absolutely honest...": BR to RR, Oct. 27, 1932, DR.

88 "When I was unrighteous...": RR to BR, Nov. 1, 1932, DR.

CHAPTER 11: A Correspondence School for Breaking Hearts

89 "For almost a decade...": BR to Theodore Schroeder, Aug. 26, 1942, SIUC.

Page

89 "simply devoid of principle.": MO to BR, Jan. 19, 1933, DR.

90 "To read the sometimes sappy...": quote by Alix Kates Shulman on book jacket of Falk, *Love, Anarchy, and Emma Goldman*.

91 "From my earliest childhood...": EO to BR, n.d., [1935], DR.

91 "plain, quiet and unassuming": Dorothy Reitman, May, 1989 and Elmer Gertz, May, 1986, personal communication.

91 "Surely you have not started...": Uno to BR, n.d., DR.

91-95 All of letters from BR to EO written between Feb. 18 and March 30, 1933 are from Dorothy Reitman's collection.

95 "I slipped my hand into the Bible...": EO to BR, [April, 1935], DR.

95 "And don't worry, my Ben.": EO to BR, [Mar 27], 1933, DR.

95-96 "he had never prayed so earnestly...": BR to EO, March 30, 1933, DR.

96 "Eileen, Eileen, look the doves...": BR to EO, March 18, 1933, DR.

96 "Someone once said...": BR to My beloved staff of the CSFTPOVD, July 20, 1938, UIC.

96 "You know when we faced each other...": EO to BR, [April 1, 1936], DR.

CHAPTER 12: Choosing the Good Sower

97 "Medina and I had a lovely romance.": BR to Theodore Schroeder, Aug. 26, 1942, SIUC.

97 "Dear Dr. Reitman:...": MO to BR, Jan. 15, 1933, DR.

98 "It would be the nicest thing...": MO to BR, Jan. 27, 1933, DR.

98 "life and love will be generous to me...": MO to BR, Jan. 19, 1933, DR.

99 "This place has three ambulances...": MO to BR, Jan. 19, 1933, DR.

Page

99 "I have never told them...": MO to BR, n.d., [1933], DR.

99 "They are well meaning simple people...": MO to BR, May 24, 1933, DR.

99 "You have a sort of natural feeling...": MO to BR, Jan. 19, 1933, RF.

99 "What/ is needed now is great souls...": BR to MO, Jan. 26, 1933, DR.

100 "I think it is a stage...": MO to BR, n.d., [1934], DR.

101 "There is a minute before duty.": MO to BR, Nov. 8, 1933, RF.

CHAPTER 13: At Least Three Women in a Lather

102 "I have to stop writing so many women...": BR to EO, [Jan., 1934], DR.

102 "I have been so crowded with visitors...": BR to EO, April 4, 1933, DR.

103 "Glad that Margaret is recovering.": BR to EO, April 5, 1933, DR.

103 "I am so sorry to have to say...": BR to EO, April 6, 1933, DR.

103 "a call to Duty..."; "We have to be mighty careful...": BR to EO, [April 8] 1933, DR.

103 "You are not an intellectual...": BR to EO, April 19, 1933, DR.

104 "I hope your new secretary...": MO to BR, April 23, 1933, DR.

104 "satiating him with sex...": EO to BR, [June, 1936], DR.

104 "We'll even pay off Rose...": EO to BR, [Nov., 1933], DR.

104 "It has been my observation tho...": MO to BR, June 2, 1933, RF.

105 "I had thought at your age and experience...": MO to BR, Dec. 21, 1933, DR.

105-106 "You certainly have not changed.": EG to BR, Dec. 23, 1933, UIC.

Page

106   "But, whether true or not...": BR to EG, BR to EG,
      Jan. 31, 1934, IISH, cited in Falk, *Love, Anarchy, and
      Emma Goldman*, 422.

106-107   "Dear Eileen, you gave me too much...": BR to EO,
          Jan. 27, 1934, DR.

107   "You will have to be careful...": BR to EG, Feb. 26, 1934,
      DR.

107   "You are never happy unless...": MO to BR, n.d., [1935],
      DR.

107   "I don't care for a resurrection of my past...": EG to
      Bennie Capes, Jan. 11, 1934, IISH, cited in Falk, *Love,
      Anarchy, and Emma Goldman*, 421.

108   "the best and most understanding letter...": BR to EG,
      April 14, 1934, IISH, Ibid., 424.

108   "still guarding me from women": BR to unknown,
      Feb. 28, 1934, DR.

108   "Different vibrations, pathological chemistry...": BR to
      unknown, April 4, 1934, DR.

108-109   "I've been so stubborn...": EO to BR, [April, 1934], DR.

109   "the two most perfect weeks of his life": BR to EO,
      May 15, 1934, DR.

109   "This afternoon while I was juggling...": MO to BR,
      May 14, 1934, DR.

109   "her word to Rose that she will bend...": MO to BR,
      [Aug., 1934], RF.

110   "How dare you suggest...": EO to BR, [June, 1934], DR.

111   "I know what I want to do...": MO to BR, June 20, 1934,
      DR.

111   "more in love with my wife now...": BR to MO,
      Aug. 4, 1934, DR.

112   "A novel appears as ridiculous for you...": MO to BR,
      Aug. 16, 1934, RF.

112   "Medina has money...": MO to BR, [Aug., 1934], RF.

113   "Even in these perilous economic times...": MO to BR,
      [Aug., 1934], RF.

113   "I love you. I want to be with you.": MO to BR,
      [Aug., 1934], RF.

Page

113   "with tears..."; "You were in such pain...": EO to BR,
      [April, 1935], DR.

114   "the vase that held..."; "It is self evident...": RR to BR,
      Oct. 29, 1934, RF.

114   "sane, wise constructive...": RR to BR, Nov. 1, 1934, RF.

114-115   "I can only hope...": EG to BR, Oct. 23, 1934, UIC.

115-116   "Servants, Sewers and Saviors", BR to EG and others,
      IISH.

116   "It's the most honest and shameless...": Jo to BR, n.d.
      [Dec. 1934], DR.

CHAPTER 14: Medina is the Promised Land

117   "There is nothing to feel bad about.": BR to MO,
      May 1, 1935, DR.

117   "fecal increment"; "public nuisance"; "If I see any
      order...": [Oct. 1934], DR.

117   "I am not able to help you...": MO to BR, Nov. 26, 1934,
      DR.

118   "If you could invest $150...": BR to Bert Lippincott,
      Jan. 11, 1935, DR.

118   "Everything that has been a real contribution...": MO to
      BR, Dec. 14, 1934, DR.

118-119   "Marge believes you have a good story...": Nels Anderson
      to BR, March 18, 1935, DR.

119   "I think she mentioned to you...": BR to Bert
      Lippencott, March 17, 1936, DR.

119   "You are much younger, dear Ben...": EG to BR,
      Dec. 5, 1934, UIC, cited in Falk, *Love, Anarchy, and
      Emma Goldman*, 439.

119   "women who have never borne children...": MO to BR,
      [Nov. 1934], DR.

119   "Ben honey, Your suggestion...": MO to BR,
      Dec. 12, 1934, DR.

120   "I feel so helpless...": MO to BR, April 25, 1935, DR.

120   "I want to get away...": BR to Brutus Reitman,
      April 27, 1935, DR.

Page

120   "Your description of your abortion...": MO to BR,
       May 30, 1935, DR.

121   "I wish it were possible...": MO to BR, May 28, 1935,
       DR.

121   "Business continues very slow.": BR to MO,
       May 30, 1935, DR.

121   "I am unable to stomach Jewish bitterness.": MO to BR,
       n.d., [1935], DR.

122   "Other people's letters...": BR to MO, [July, 1935], DR.

122-123 "I will always remember...": MO to BR, [August, 1935],
       DR.

123   Darling, I don't want to get...": BR to MO, Aug. 8, 1935,
       DR.

123   "I pine and long for Medina...": BR to Brutus Reitman,
       [summer, 1935], DR.

123   "I'm still fond of you...": Jo to BR, n.d. [1935], DR.

123-124 "You have my number...": BR to MO, Oct. 11, 1935, DR.

124   "Gen Coxey...made a great talk...": BR to unknown,
       Oct. 16, 1935, DR.

124   "Under separate cover...": MO to BR, n.d., [1935], DR.

125   "Consider this two dollars...": MO to BR,
       March 17, 1936, DR.

125   "Every so often you write me something...": MO to BR,
       Aug. 12, 1934, DR.

125   "It is better that she suffer...": BR to June,
       March 17, 1936, DR.

126   "I am glad you want to sleep...": EO to BR, n.d., [1935],
       DR.

126   "I have never had a home.": EO to BR, n.d., [1935], DR.

127   "My greatness must develop...": EO to BR, n.d., [1935],
       DR.

127   "The spirit of it all...": EO to BR, n.d., [1935], DR.

127   "Two years ago today...": EO to BR, June [1935], DR.

127   "I never have the slightest doubt...": BR to EO,
       July 18, 1936, DR.

127   "Chance brought me to you...": EO to BR, April, [1935],
       DR.

Page

128   "Your plans are large...": MO to BR, n.d., [1936], DR.

128-129 "and give you my frank and sympathetic...": EG to BR, April 27, 1936, UIC, cited in Falk, *Love, Anarchy, and Emma Goldman*, 468.

129   "until the others have gotten through...": MO to BR, n.d., 1934, DR.

129   "If you want to be famous...": MO to BR, March 3, 1936, DR.

129   "Medina on the left...": MO to BR, n.d., [1936], DR.

130   "Things are sure...": MO to BR, n.d., [1936], DR.

CHAPTER 15: It is All So Delightful, So Interesting

131   "The beautiful thing about life...": BR to Herbert Blumer, Dec. 7, 1936, DR.

131   "I must have some place to work...": MO to BR, May 27, [1936], DR.

132   "Darling Ben, I'm still menstruating...": EO to BR April n.d., [1936], DR.

132   "the Madonna with child': BR to "Blue Eyes", July 3, 1936, UIC.

132   "Eileen thinks that because of Medina...": BR to Brutus Reitman, Aug. 1, 1936, DR.

133   "of a pregnant woman...": EO Diary, 1936, DR.

133   "God tells me to stay...": Ibid.

133   "20 years in the future.": EO to BR, n.d. [1935], DR.

134   "I want to do certain work...": "Jo" to BR, n.d., Jan. 1 [1934], DR.

134   "I am expecting the Madonna...": BR to Jan Gay and Brutus Reitman, Aug. 7, 1936, DR.

135   "5:50 PM. Today I saw three pregnant women...": BR to unknown, Sept. 23, 1936, DR.

136   "I have not forgot you...": "Helen" to BR, March 19, 1940, UIC.

136   "The record of Mecca Benn Reitman's birth...": MO to Leo A. Ozies, May 1, 1957, RF.

Page

138   "If you have changed your plans...": Inez Oliver to MO
      n.d., [1936], RF.

138   "Patients, Poets, Sociologists...": EO Diary, 1936, DR.

138   "Take care of yourself...": Ibid.

138   "I will be remembered by my carbons...": BR to
      unknown, n.d., [1936], DR.

139   "We can imagine terrible things...": Inez Oliver to MO,
      n.d., [1936], RF.

139   "We all make mistakes...": Eugene Oliver to MO, Ibid.

140   "There are seventy other women...": MO to BR,
      [Dec., 1936], DR.

140   "Do not be disturbed...": MO to BR, [Dec.,1936], DR.

140-141 "If the lie of the assumed name...": Inez Oliver to MO,
      [Dec., 1936], RF.

141   "Oh my darling, won't you try...": BR to MO, [Dec., 1936], DR.

141   "how you wish us to address you...": Eugene Oliver to
      MO, [Dec., 1936], RF.

142-143 "Most of the neighborhood...": BR to Eugene Oliver,
      Jan. 16, 1937, DR.

143   "It would take a consummate artist...": BR to Jan Gay
      and Marie Thompson, Jan. 2, 1937, DR.

144   "I have plenty of time you would think...": MO to BR,
      [Dec., 1936], DR.

144   "great courage, I'm sure.": EO diary, 1936, DR.

144   "Ben says I shall see Mecca...": Ibid.

144-145 "Why can't I act when I know...": Ibid.

145   "the best Christmas and New Years..."; "He thought
      of me..."; "How hurt I have always felt...": Ibid.

145   "Aren't we good enough for her?": Ibid.

145   "Medina just plays with Mecca...": Ibid.

145   "We fixed up Box Car Bertha": Ibid.

146   My father's book was published under the title *Sister of
      the Road: The Autobiography of Box-Car Bertha*, as told to
      Dr. Ben L. Reitman, New York: The Macaulay Company,
      1937. It has been reprinted as *Boxcar Bertha: An Auto-
      biography* as told to Dr. Ben L. Reitman, New York:
      Amok Press, 1988.

Page

146-147   "That is the 'Gift of the Gods'...": BR to Leo Furman,
           Nov. 3, 1936, DR.

           CHAPTER 15: Soap and Water

   148   "We must make sex safe, foolproof.": BR, VDC 96, 508,
          UIC.
   148   "the old mommy is no more."; "It is you who are
          dead...": EG to BR, n.d., [1933], UIC.
   149   A full description of venereal disease and its treatment
          from 1920-1940 is in Brandt, *No Magic Bullet*, Chap. 4.
   150   "Chicago has the largest and best..."; "Gentlemen, I
          realize that...": BR to Drs. Bundesen, Schmidt and
          Taylor, Dec. 24, 1936, DR.
   152   "Can you catch syphilis...": BR, "Syphilis in My Life",
          Phoenix 18, 1937, 28.
   152   "Syphilis is a venereal disease...": *Help Stamp Out
          Syphilis*, Chicago Medical Society and Chicago Health
          Department, 1938, UIC.
   152   "You can become infected by having sex...": *Under-
          standing AIDS*, The Surgeon General and the Centers for
          Disease Control, U.S. Public Health Service, 1988.
   153   "The procedure for prevention...": BR, "Syphilis in My
          Life", *Phoenix* 18, 1937, 28.
   153   "If you can't be moral...": Suzanne Poirier, *Chicago's War
          on Syphilis*, 29.
   153   "We're going to do it...": BR, VDC ?, 550, UIC.
   154   "You can't teach people...": BR, VDC 97, 511, UIC.
   154   "It is the utmost importance...": Thomas Parran, Jr.,
          Shadow on the Land: Syphilis, New York, Reynal and
          Hitchcock, 1937, cited in Poirier, *Chicago's War on
          Syphilis*, 82-83.
   154   "How can you tell if...": BR, VDC 39, 220, UIC.
   154   "We believe a time will come...": BR, VDC 48, 206,
          UIC.
   155   "Clinics and treatments will never solve...": BR,
          VDC 36, 219, UIC.

Page

155   "Everyone agrees that prophylaxis...": BR to William A. Evans, April 8, 1938, UIC.

155   "Our talk on syphilis control...": BR, VDC 158, 765, UIC.

155-156   "I Was Walking..."; "There's more colored people...: BR, VDC 143, 715, UIC.

156   "the Wasserman dragnet": Brandt, *No Magic Bullet*, 139.

156-157   "The Syphilis Control Program...": BR, VDC 302, 411, UIC.

157   "not to be so vulgar and sexy...": BR, VDC 203,   1000, UIC.

157   "Unto the lewd...": BR, VDC, Ibid.

157   "If this town...": BR, VDC 124, 612, UIC.

157-158   "a group of Gary women"; "some of the Bohemian places...": Verrain Dilley to BR, March 11, 1940, UIC.

158   "When people become enlightened...": BR, VDC 50, 304, UIC.

158   "I'm sorry I can't do it"; "The clergy, the women's clubs...": VDC 333, 1723, UIC.

158-159   "What would you say if...": Ibid.

159   "Schmidt was genial...": BR to Lawrence Linck, Nov. 13, 1938, UIC.

159   "there are two members..."; "There are several valid reasons...": Ibid.

CHAPTER 17: I Pass on Life to My Children

160   "Through my children...": BR to unknown, May 3, 1940, UIC.

160   "liar, thief, betrayer of young girls"; "You can imagine all the things...": BR to Theodore Schroeder, Dec., 1937, UIC.

161   "Rose visited Grandpa Oliver...": n.d., wedding invitation, 1937, UIC.

161   "Mother looks just like she is...": BR to Eugene and Inez Oliver, Jan. 20, 1938, UIC.

162   "Brave Medina who stands by me": BR to Jan Gay, August n.d., [1937], UIC.

Page

162   "I doubt if ever Mother was more anxious...": BR to
       Eugene and Inez Oliver, Oct. 12, 1938, UIC.

163   "It is a surprise to us...": MO to BR, [Nov. 1938], UIC.

163   "I wake up so often in the night...": BR to MO,
       Nov. 7, 1938, UIC.

164   "You have been one of my...": Nels Anderson to BR,
       Nov. 23, 1938, UIC.

164   "or two or three books": BR to Lee Furman,
       Nov. 14, 1938, UIC.

164   "Poor dear Mother was so timid...": BR to Eugene and
       Inez Oliver, Dec. 7, 1938, UIC.

164   "People who have confidence...": BR to Eugene Oliver,
       [Jan. 1939], UIC.

165   "Yes Dear Medina, Dad is not the only one...": BR to
       MO, Jan. 17, 1939, UIC.

166   "vicissitudes of a vaccinator"; "Frequently we see
       newspapermen...": BR, Weekly Report 3,
       March 22, 1939, UIC.

166   "direct action and sabotage": BR to William Evans,
       April 15, 1939, UIC.

166   "oblivion, melancholy and suicide": BR to Brutus
       Reitman, Aug. 18, 1939, UIC.

166   "Don't expect me to visit you..."; "Jail, death and
       infamy...": Ibid.

167   "To me the book is largely fiction...": Preface to "Ben
       Reitman Tale" (Clown of Glory), Milton and Gertz, UIC.
       Elmer Gertz was also helpful with many events relating
       to his manuscript.

167-168 "For a man who swears by Jesus...": EG to BR,
       June 29, 1939, UIC, cited in Falk, *Love, Anarchy,
       and Emma Goldman*, 496.

168   "Sometimes I think I am better..."; "Betty's poor judge
       ment...": BR to Brutus Reitman, March 18, 1939, UIC.

168-169 "I felt all along...": EG to BR, Nov. 22, 1939, UIC.

169   "The practice of medicine is humiliating...": BR to
       William Evans, Dec. 9, 1939, UIC.

Page

169   "She has been my secretary...": BR to Jan Gay, Feb. 12, 1940, UIC.

169-170   "I hope you will rejoice...": BR to unknown, May 3, 1940, UIC.

170   "This is my little Emma Goldman.": Lila Weinberg, personal communication, Jan. 1991.

170   "She was so sorry to lose her job...": BR to Theodore Schroeder, May 21, 1940, SIUC.

170   "Life is a series of choices...": MO to BR, [May, 1940], UIC.

170   "We love you very much...": MO to BR, [May, 1940], UIC.

170-171   "As long as life lasts...": BR to MO, June 20, 1940, UIC.

171   "I hope they [your family] ain't worried...": BR to MO, June 22, 1940, UIC.

171   "I have two lovely babies...": BR to RR, Aug. 1, 1940, UIC.

171   "My glorious Irish Queen...": Ibid.

171-172   "I loved Medina...": BR to Theodore Schroeder, Aug. 24, 1942, SIUC.

173   "Today millions of men...": BR to Theodore Schroeder, [Oct.] 24, 1940, SIUC.

178   "We took the car...": BR to Brutus Reitman, Sept. 5, 1941, UIC.

173-174   "My time on earth is limited...": BR to Brutus Reitman, Sept. 29, 1941, UIC.

174   "I do hope you can live...": BR to Brutus Reitman, Dec. 13, 1941, UIC.

174   "I've been having a most thrilling...": BR to Brutus Reitman, Feb. 10, 1942, UIC.

171   "So now Medina has three little girls...": BR to Brutus Reitman and Jan Gay, Feb. 19, 1942, UIC.

174   "As you would expect...": BR to Brutus Reitman, Feb. 23, 1942, UIC.

175   "I...made the same mistake..."; "Thanks to a few friends...": BR to William Evans, June 22, 1942, UIC.

Page

175   "But all in all...": BR to Inez Oliver, Nov. 2, 1942, UIC.

175-176"Ben Lewis Reitman, M.D., died...": MO, [Nov., 1942],
           RF.

176   "Stop all legal proceedings of will...": newsclipping,
           [Nov. 17, 1942], UIC, RF.

CHAPTER 18: Living My Father's Life

177   "LIFE has always been wonderful...": BR, "Reveries
           at Sixty", [January, 1939], UIC.

177   "I am hoping Mecca will want to know me.": BR to
           Brutus Reitman, Aug. 12, 1936, DR.

178   "It took three families...": BR to Jan Gay, Feb. 8, 1939,
           UIC.

179   "You are better and more developed...": BR to MO,
           May 1, 1935, DR.

179   "You see, sweet, I love you...": MO to BR, Dec. 30, 1933,
           DR.

Selected Reading

The following books have been my guides in searching for my father:

Bruns, Roger. *The Damndest Radical: The Life and World of Ben Reitman, Chicago's Celebrated Social Reformer, Hobo King, and Whorehouse Physician*, Urbana: University of Illinois Press, 1987

Falk, Candace. *Love, Anarchy, and Emma Goldman*, New York: Holt, Rinehart and Winston, 1984; rev. ed., New Brunswick: Rutgers University Press, 1990

Goldman, Emma. *Living My Life*, Vol. I and Vol. II, New York: Dover, 1970

Poirer, Suzanne. *Chicago's War on Syphilis, 1937-1940; The Times, The Trib and the Clap Doctor*, Urbana: University of Illinois Press, 1995

Shulman, Alix Kates. "Living Our Life," in *Between Women* (L. De Salvo, S. Ruddick, eds.), Boston: Beacon Press, 1984

Wexler, Alice. *Emma Goldman: An Intimate Life*, New York: Pantheon Books, 1984

————. *Emma Goldman in Exile*, Boston: Beacon Press, 1989

Evocative of the period that Emma and Ben were together are the bound volumes of *Mother Earth* (1906-1918) located in the Newberry Library in Chicago, across the street from Bughouse

Square where Ben used to speak.

Finally, for readers like me who enjoy the intimacy of reading other people's mail, I commend you to the collections of Ben's and Emma's papers:

The Ben L. Reitman Papers, located at the University of Illinois at Chicago, The University Library, Department of Special Collections is a treasure trove containing Ben's letters and those of his correspondents, his unpublished autobiography, "Following the Monkey," his Venereal Disease Control Reports and a vast store of related materials.

The Emma Goldman Papers Project at the University of California, Berkeley has assembled Emma's letters, writings, government surveillance and legal documents and newsclippings from libraries and collections worldwide. *Emma Goldman Papers: A Microfilm Edition*, Alexandria: Chadwyck-Healey, Inc, 1991, and its companion volume, *Emma Goldman: A Guide to Her Life and Documentary Sources*, Alexandria: Chadwyck-Healey, 1995 are available at libraries across the US and around the world. You may locate those libraries and preview selected material at the award winning webside: http://sunsite.berkeley.edu/Goldman.

Index

About the Author

MECCA REITMAN CARPENTER has been a scientist, a health writer, a teacher and a fundraiser. She is the editor of *The Culinary Kid: A Nutrition Guide & Cookbook for Parents & Kids*. She lives in California and works in Development Research at California State Polytechnic University, Pomona.

Books published by SouthSide Press are available at quantity discounts on bulk purchases for premium, educational, fundraising and special sales use. For information, please contact:

SOUTHSIDE PRESS
94 Pleasant Street, Lexington, MA 02421
Fax: (781) 862-4027, Phone: (800) 378-8711